Readings for Holy Week

Book design: Sandy Fay,
Laughing Horse Graphics, Quakertown, PA

Cover photos: Comstock Klips and Digital Stock. Used by permission.

Chapter artwork: C.I. Publishing, 800.353.2225. Used by permission.

ISBN 1-878422-47-2 Hardcover
ISBN 1-878422-48-0 Large Print Hardcover
ISBN 1-878422-49-9 Hardcover with Music

Printed in the United States of America

ℐoreward

Readings for Holy Week represents a harmony account of the sufferings, death, resurrection and ascension of the Lord Jesus Christ as it is found in the New Testament. Its roots go back nearly 250 years to the Moravian Church in Germany, where the first copy of *The Story of the Days of the Son of Man, compiled from the Four Gospels* (translated title) was printed for individual devotional use.

In 1771 the manuscript was first translated into English, using the King James version of the Bible. Diaries of early American Moravian settlements indicate these readings — known then as the *Passion Week Manual* — were used congregationally: Ministers read daily to their congregations portions of the account, which was divided to reflect Christ's activities during each day of holy week. Songs reflecting the rich musical traditions of Moravians accompanied the service. In the 1930s, these music stanzas were inserted into the text, creating the format now used throughout North America.

This version of *Readings for Holy Week* is based on the NRSV translation of the Bible. In order to present a text suitable for public reading, some editing, including the deletion of repetitions, has been necessary.

Hymn stanzas have been included at appropriate points in the readings. For the most part these are hymns sanctioned by long established usage in these services. The number at the top left of each hymn indicates the location of the tune in the 1995 edition of the *Moravian Book of Worship.* (The designation at the top right refers to a metrical arrangement by Christian Gregor of hymn tunes used in the Moravian Church.) A hymn number with an R indicates a tune found in the *Hymnal and Liturgies of the Moravian Church, 1969.*

A boxed number in the margin indicates the page on which the nearby hymn or text appears in the 1995 edition of *Readings for Holy Week* without music.

Even though the language and hymns have been updated, the rich Moravian tradition of devotion to Christ and reflection on his willing sacrifice on the cross remains — timeless and unchanging.

Saturday

The Anointing at Bethany
Mark 14:5-9; John 11:55-12:11

5   Now the Passover of the Jews was near, and many went up from the country to Jerusalem before the Passover to purify themselves. They were looking for Jesus and were asking one another as they stood in the temple, "What do you think? Surely he will not come to the festival, will he?" Now the chief priests and the Pharisees had given orders that anyone who knew where Jesus was should let them know, so that they might arrest him.

Six days before the Passover Jesus came to Bethany, the home of Lazarus, whom he had raised from the dead. There they gave a dinner for him in the house of Simon the leper. Martha served, and Lazarus was one of those at the table with him.

Mary took a pound of costly perfume made of pure nard, anointed Jesus' feet, and wiped them with her hair. The house was filled with the fragrance of the perfume.

A - noint me with your heav'n - ly grace, a -
dopt me for your own, that I may see your
glo - rious face and wor - ship at your throne.

C.M.
EVAN

6 But Judas Iscariot, one of his disciples (the one who was about to betray him), said, "Why was this perfume not sold for three hundred denarii and the money given to the poor?" (He said this not because he cared about the poor, but because he was a thief; he kept the common purse and used to steal what was put into it.) And the other disciples scolded Mary.

But Jesus said, "Let her alone; why do you trouble her? She has performed a good service for me. For you always have the poor with you, and you can show kindness to them whenever you wish; but you will not always have me. She has done what she could; she has anointed my body beforehand for its burial. Truly I tell you, wherever the good news is proclaimed in the whole world, what she has done will be told in remembrance of her."

Je - sus, Mas - ter, whom I serve, though so feeb - ly and so ill, strength-en hand and heart and nerve, all your bid - ding to ful - fill; o - pen now my eyes to see all the work you have for me.

7.7.7.7.7.7. Trochaic
GRACEHAM (581 K)

7 When the great crowd of the Jews learned that Jesus was there, they came not only because of him but also to see Lazarus, whom he had raised from the dead. So the chief priests planned to put Lazarus to death as well, since it was on account of him that many of the Jews were deserting and were believing in Jesus.

Sunday

The Triumphal Entry
Matthew 21:4-5, 9; Mark 11:1-8;
Luke 19:37-40; John 12:12,16

8 | The next day as Jesus and his disciples were approaching Jerusalem, at Bethphage and Bethany, near the Mount of Olives, Jesus sent two of his disciples and said to them, "Go into the village ahead of you, and immediately as you enter it, you will find tied there a colt that has never been ridden; untie it and bring it. If anyone says to you, 'Why are you doing this?' just say this, 'The Lord needs it and will send it back here immediately.' "

They went away and found a colt tied near a door, outside in the street. As they were untying it, some of the bystanders said to them, "What are you doing, untying the colt?" They told them what Jesus had said; and they allowed them to take it. Then they brought the colt to Jesus and threw their cloaks on it; and he sat on it.

The great crowd that had come to the festival heard that Jesus was coming to Jerusalem, and many people spread their cloaks on the road, and others spread leafy branches that they had cut in the fields.

9

Hail to the Lord's A - noint - ed, great Da-vid's great-er Son!

Hail in the time ap - point - ed, his reign on earth be - gun!

He comes to break op - pres - sion, to set the cap-tive free,

to take a-way trans - gres - sion, and rule in eq - ui - ty.

7.6.7.6.D. Iambic
ST. THEODULPH (151 G)

As Jesus was now approaching the path down from the Mount of Olives, the whole multitude of the disciples began to praise God joyfully with a loud voice for all the deeds of power that they had seen, shouting,

"Hosanna to the Son of David!
Blessed is the one who comes
in the name of the Lord!
Hosanna in the highest heaven!"

239 ∽ The Hosanna

10 His disciples did not understand these things at first; but when Jesus was glorified, then they remembered that these things had been written of him and had been done to him. This took place to fulfill what had been spoken through the prophet, saying, "Tell the daughter of Zion, look, your king is coming to you, humble, and mounted on a donkey, on a colt, the foal of a donkey."

```
1 Ride   on!  Ride   on   in   maj - es - ty!  Hear
2 Ride   on!  Ride   on   in   maj - es - ty!  Your
3 Ride   on!  Ride   on   in   maj - es - ty!  In
```

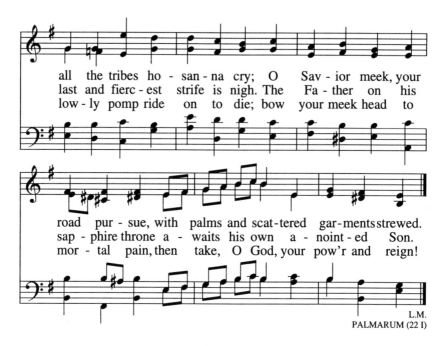

all the tribes ho - san - na cry; O Sav - ior meek, your
last and fierc - est strife is nigh. The Fa - ther on his
low - ly pomp ride on to die; bow your meek head to

road pur - sue, with palms and scat-tered gar-ments strewed.
sap - phire throne a - waits his own a - noint - ed Son.
mor - tal pain, then take, O God, your pow'r and reign!

L.M.
PALMARUM (22 I)

Some of the Pharisees in the crowd said to him, "Teacher, order your disciples to stop." He answered, "I tell you, if these were silent, the stones would shout out."

Ho - san - na, our glad voic - es raise, Ho -

san - na to our King! Should we for - get our

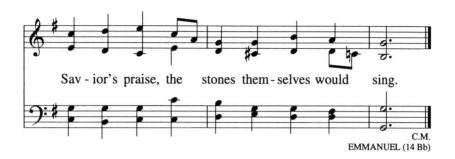

Sav - ior's praise, the   stones them - selves would   sing.

C.M.
EMMANUEL (14 Bb)

Jesus Weeps over Jerusalem
Matthew 21:10-16; Luke 19:41-44;
John 12:19

11 As Jesus came near and saw the city, he wept over it, saying, "If you, even you, had only recognized on this day the things that make for peace! But now they are hidden from your eyes. Indeed, the days will come upon you, when your enemies will set up ramparts around you and surround you, and hem you in on every side. They will crush you to the ground, you and your children within you, and they will not leave within you one stone upon another; because you did not recognize the time of your visitation from God."

When Jesus entered Jerusalem, the whole city was in turmoil, asking, "Who is this?"

The crowds were saying, "This is the prophet Jesus from Nazareth in Galilee."

The Pharisees then said to one another, "You see, you can do nothing. Look, the world has gone after him!"

O that with yon-der sa-cred throng we at his feet may

fall; we'll join the ev-er-last-ing song, and

crown him Lord of all! We'll join the ev-er-

last-ing song, and crown him Lord of all!

C.M.
CORONATION (14 R)

12 Then Jesus entered the temple and the blind and the lame came to him, and he cured them. But when the chief priests and the scribes saw the amazing things that he did, and heard the children crying out in the temple, "Hosanna to the Son of David," they became angry and said to him, "Do you hear what these are saying?"

Jesus said to them, "Yes; have you never read, 'Out of the mouths of infants and nursing babies you have prepared praise for yourself'?"

All glo-ry, laud, and hon-or to you, Re-deem-er, King,
to whom the lips of chil-dren made sweet ho-san-nas ring.
You are the King of Is-ra-el and Da-vid's roy-al Son,
now in the Lord's name com-ing, the King and Bless-ed One.

7.6.7.6.D. Iambic
ST. THEODULPH (151 G)

Jesus Speaks about His Death
Mark 11:11; John 12:20-36

Now among those who went up to worship at the festival were some Greeks. They came to Philip, who was from Bethsaida in Galilee, and said to him, "Sir, we wish to see Jesus." Philip went and told Andrew; then Andrew and Philip went and told Jesus.

13 Jesus answered them, "The hour has come for the Son of Man to be glorified. Very truly, I tell you, unless a grain of wheat falls into the earth and dies, it remains just a single grain; but if it dies, it bears much fruit. Those who love their life lose it, and those who hate their life in this world will keep it for eternal life. Whoever serves me must follow me, and where I am, there will my servant be also. Whoever serves me, the Father will honor."

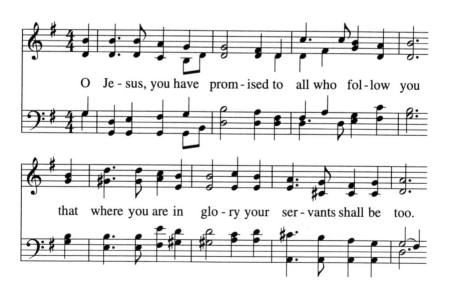

O Je - sus, you have prom - ised to all who fol - low you

that where you are in glo - ry your ser - vants shall be too.

And Je-sus, I have prom-ised to serve you to the end;

O give me grace to fol-low, my mas-ter and my friend.

7.6.7.6.D.
ANGEL'S STORY

"Now my soul is troubled. And what should I say — 'Father, save me from this hour'? No, it is for this reason that I have come to this hour. Father, glorify your name."

Then a voice came from heaven, "I have glorified it, and I will glorify it again."

The crowd standing there heard it and said that it was thunder. Others said, "An angel has spoken to him."

14 Jesus answered, "This voice has come for your sake, not for mine. Now is the judgment of this world; now the ruler of this world will be driven out. And I, when I am lifted up from the earth, will draw all people to myself." He said this to indicate the kind of death he was to die.

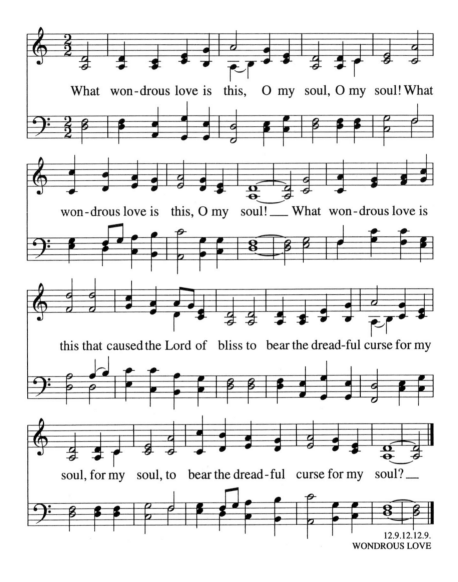

What won-drous love is this, O my soul, O my soul! What won-drous love is this, O my soul! ___ What won-drous love is this that caused the Lord of bliss to bear the dread-ful curse for my soul, for my soul, to bear the dread-ful curse for my soul? ___

12.9.12.12.9.
WONDROUS LOVE

The crowd answered him, "We have heard from the law that the Messiah remains forever. How can you say that the Son of Man must be lifted up? Who is this Son of Man?"

Jesus said to them, "The light is with you for a little longer. Walk while you have the light, so that the darkness may not overtake you. If you walk in the darkness, you do not know where you are going. While you have the light, believe in the light, so that you may become children of light."

When sim - pli - ci - ty we cher - ish, then the soul is full of light; but that light will quick - ly van - ish, when of Je - sus we lose sight.

8.7.8.7. Trochaic
BATTY (16 A)

As it was already late, he went out to Bethany with the twelve.

Beth-a-ny, O peace-ful hab-i - ta-tion, bless-ed man-sion,

loved a - bode; there my Lord had oft his rest-ing sta-tion,

con-verse held in friend-ly mood: with that bliss which Mar-y high-ly

sav-ored, I could wish this day still to be fav-ored;

but his pres-ence makes to me ev-'ry place a Beth-a - ny.

10.7.10.7.10.10.7.7.
COVENANT (185 A)

20

$\mathcal{M}$onday

Jesus Curses the Fig Tree
Mark 11:12-14

16 On the following day, when they came from Bethany, Jesus was hungry. Seeing in the distance a fig tree in leaf, he went to see whether perhaps he would find anything on it. When he came to it, he found nothing but leaves, for it was not the season for figs. He said to it, "May no one ever eat fruit from you again." And his disciples heard it.

Jesus Cleanses the Temple
Mark 11:15-19

Then they came to Jerusalem. And Jesus entered the temple and began to drive out those who were selling and those who were buying in the temple, and he overturned the tables of the money changers and the seats of those who sold doves; and he would not allow anyone to carry anything through the temple.

He was teaching and saying, "Is it not written, 'My house shall be called a house of prayer for all the nations'? But you have made it a den of robbers."

17 And when the chief priests and the scribes heard it, they kept looking for a way to kill him; for they were afraid of him, because the whole crowd was spellbound by his teaching. And when evening came, Jesus and his disciples went out of the city.

1 To your tem - ple, Lord, I come,
2 From your house when I re - turn,

for it is my wor - ship home. This earth has no
may my heart with - in me burn, and at eve - ning

bet - ter place, here I see my Sav - ior's face.
let me say, "I have walked with God to - day."

7.7.7.7. Trochaic
HERRNHUT (11 A)

Tuesday

The Lesson from the
Withered Fig Tree
Mark 11:20-25

18 In the morning as they passed by, they saw the fig tree withered away to its roots. Then Peter remembered and said to him, "Rabbi, look! The fig tree that you cursed has withered."

Jesus answered them, "Have faith in God. Truly I tell you, if you say to this mountain, 'Be taken up and thrown into the sea,' and if you do not doubt in your heart, but believe that what you say will come to pass, it will be done for you. So I tell you, whatever you ask for in prayer, believe that you have received it, and it will be yours.

"Whenever you stand praying, forgive, if you have anything against anyone; so that your Father in heaven may also forgive you your trespasses."

1 Par - don, Lord, and are there those
2 Much for - giv - en, may I learn

who my debt - ors are, or foes? I, who by for -
love for ha - tred to re - turn; then my heart as -

give - ness live, here their tres - pass - es for - give.
sured shall be you, my God, have par - doned me.

7.7.7.7. Trochaic
HERRNHUT (11 A)

The Authority of Jesus Questioned
Matthew 21:23-27

19 When Jesus entered the temple, the chief priests and the elders of the people came to him as he was teaching, and said, "By what authority are you doing these things, and who gave you this authority?"

Jesus said to them, "I will also ask you one question; if you tell me the answer, then I will also tell you by what authority I do these things. Did the baptism of John come from heaven, or was it of human origin?"

And they argued with one another, "If we say, 'From heaven,' he will say to us, 'Why then did you not believe him?' But if we say, 'Of human origin,' we are afraid of the crowd; for all regard John as a prophet." So they answered Jesus, "We do not know."

And he said to them, "Neither will I tell you by what authority I am doing these things."

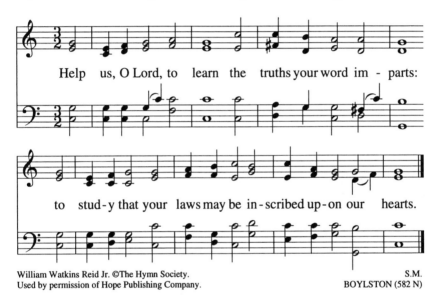

Help us, O Lord, to learn the truths your word im - parts:

to stud-y that your laws may be in-scribed up-on our hearts.

William Watkins Reid Jr. ©The Hymn Society.
Used by permission of Hope Publishing Company.

S.M.
BOYLSTON (582 N)

The Parable of the Two Sons
Matthew 21:28-32

[20] Jesus answered, "What do you think? A man had two sons; he went to the first and said, 'Son, go and work in the vineyard today.' He answered, 'I will not'; but later he changed his mind and went. The father went to the second and said the same; and he answered, 'I go, sir'; but he did not go. Which of the two did the will of his father?"

They said, "The first."

Jesus said to them, "Truly I tell you, the tax collectors and the prostitutes are going into the kingdom of God ahead of you. For John came to you in the way of righteousness and you did not believe him, but the tax collectors and the prostitutes believed him; and even after you saw it, you did not change your minds and believe him."

Help us, O God of love, to live as you de - sire.

Kin-dle re - pen-tance in our hearts, and cleanse us with your fire.

S.M.
SWABIA (582 K)

The Parable of the Vineyard
Matthew 21:33-46

21 "Listen to another parable. There was a landowner who planted a vineyard, put a fence around it, dug a wine press in it, and built a watchtower. Then he leased it to tenants and went to another country. When the harvest time had come, he

sent his slaves to the tenants to collect his produce. But the tenants seized his slaves and beat one, killed another, and stoned another. Again he sent other slaves, more than the first; and they treated them in the same way. Finally he sent his son to them, saying, 'They will respect my son.' But when the tenants saw the son, they said to themselves, 'This is the heir; come, let us kill him and get his inheritance.' So they seized him, threw him out of the vineyard, and killed him. Now when the owner of the vineyard comes, what will he do to those tenants?"

They said to him, "He will put those wretches to a miserable death, and lease the vineyard to other tenants who will give him the produce at the harvest time."

Jesus said to them, "Have you never read in the scriptures: 'The stone that the builders rejected has become the cornerstone; this was the Lord's doing, and it is amazing in our eyes'?

Therefore I tell you, the kingdom of God will be taken away from you and given to a people that produces the fruits of the kingdom."

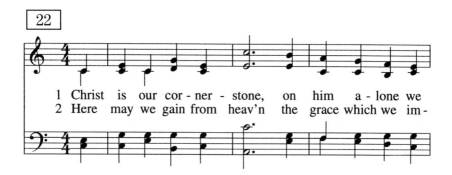

22

1 Christ is our cor - ner - stone, on him a - lone we
2 Here may we gain from heav'n the grace which we im -

build;   with   his   true saints   a - lone   the courts of
plore;   and   may that grace, once   giv'n,   be   with us

heav'n are   filled;   on   his   great   love   our
ev - er - more,   un - til   that   day   when

hopes we place of   pres - ent grace and   joys   a - bove.
all   the blessed to   end - less rest are   called   a - way!

6.6.6.6.8.8.
DARWALL (342 D)

When the chief priests and the Pharisees heard his parables, they realized that he was speaking about them. They wanted to arrest him, but they feared the crowds, because they regarded him as a prophet.

Praise the Lord, praise the Lord! He with you deals boun-teous-ly.

High-ly fa-vored church of Je-sus, he chose you through mer-cy free

to show forth his match-less prais-es and rich fruit, blessed

for the Mas-ter's use, to pro-duce, to pro-duce.

3.3.7.8.7.8.9.3.3. Trochaic
HOLY LORD (119 A)

The Parable of the Wedding Banquet
Matthew 22:1-14

23 Once more Jesus spoke to them in parables, saying: "The kingdom of heaven may be compared

to a king who gave a wedding banquet for his son. He sent his slaves to call those who had been invited to the wedding banquet, but they would not come. Again he sent other slaves, saying, 'Tell those who have been invited: Look, I have prepared my dinner, my oxen and my fat calves have been slaughtered, and everything is ready; come to the wedding banquet.' But they made light of it and went away, one to his farm, another to his business, while the rest seized his slaves, mistreated them, and killed them. The king was enraged. He sent his troops, destroyed those murderers, and burned their city. Then he said to his slaves, 'The wedding is ready, but those invited were not worthy. Go therefore into the main streets, and invite everyone you find to the wedding banquet.' "

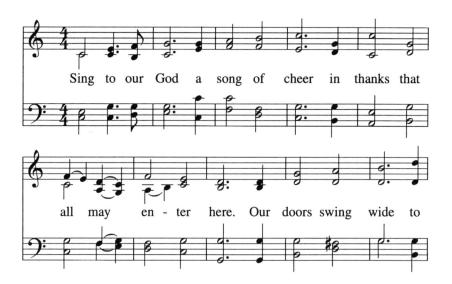

Sing to our God a song of cheer in thanks that all may en - ter here. Our doors swing wide to

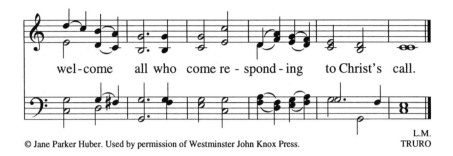

wel-come   all who come re - spond - ing   to Christ's call.

L.M.
TRURO

24 "Those slaves went out into the streets and gathered all whom they found, both good and bad; so the wedding hall was filled with guests. But when the king came in to see the guests, he noticed a man there who was not wearing a wedding robe, and he said to him, 'Friend, how did you get in here without a wedding robe?' And he was speechless. Then the king said to the attendants, 'Bind him hand and foot, and throw him into the outer darkness, where there will be weeping and gnashing of teeth.' For many are called, but few are chosen."

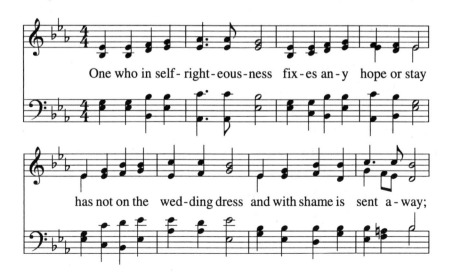

One who in self- right-eous-ness fix-es an-y hope or stay

has not on the wed-ding dress and with shame is   sent a - way;

to the hun-gry wea-ry heart God will food and rest im-part.

7.7.7.7.7.7. Trochaic
PETRA (581 G)

A Question about Paying Taxes
Matthew 22:15-22

25 Then the Pharisees went and plotted to entrap him in what he said. So they sent their disciples to him, along with the Herodians, saying, "Teacher, we know that you are sincere, and teach the way of God in accordance with truth, and show deference to no one; for you do not regard people with partiality. Tell us, then, what you think. Is it lawful to pay taxes to the emperor, or not?"

But Jesus, aware of their malice, said, "Why are you putting me to the test, you hypocrites? Show me the coin used for the tax." And they brought him a denarius.

Then he said to them, "Whose head is this, and whose title?"

They answered, "The emperor's."

Then he said to them, "Give therefore to the emperor the things that are the emperor's, and to God the things that are God's." When they heard this, they were amazed; and they left him and went away.

O Je-sus, high-est trea-sure, in your com-mun-ion blessed

I find un-fail-ing plea-sure, true hap-pi-ness and rest;

my-self a will-ing of-f'ring I give to you a-lone,

be-cause by death and suf-f'ring you did for me a-tone.

7.6.7.6.D.
MUNICH

A Question about the Resurrection
Matthew 22:23-33

26 The same day some Sadducees came to him, saying there is no resurrection; and they asked him a question, saying, "Teacher, Moses said, 'If a man

dies childless, his brother shall marry the widow, and raise up children for his brother.' Now there were seven brothers among us; the first married, and died childless, leaving the widow to his brother. The second did the same, so also the third, down to the seventh. Last of all, the woman herself died. In the resurrection, then, whose wife of the seven will she be? For all of them had married her."

Jesus answered them, "You are wrong, because you know neither the scriptures nor the power of God. For in the resurrection they neither marry nor are given in marriage, but are like angels in heaven. And as for the resurrection of the dead, have you not read what was said to you by God, 'I am the God of Abraham, the God of Isaac, and the God of Jacob'? He is God not of the dead, but of the living." And when the crowd heard it, they were astounded at his teaching.

Lord, our God, Lord, our God, may your pre-cious sav-ing word, till our days on earth are end-ed, light un-to our

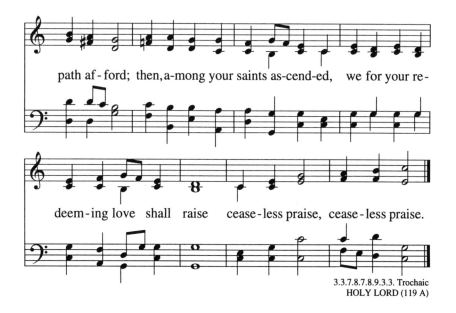

path af-ford; then, a-mong your saints as-cend-ed, we for your re-

deem-ing love shall raise cease-less praise, cease-less praise.

3.3.7.8.7.8.9.3.3. Trochaic
HOLY LORD (119 A)

The Great Commandment
Matthew 22:34-40; Mark 12:32-34

27   When the Pharisees heard that he had silenced the Sadducees, they gathered together, and one of them, a lawyer, asked him a question to test him. "Teacher, which commandment in the law is the greatest?"

He said to him, "'You shall love the Lord your God with all your heart, and with all your soul, and with all your mind.' This is the greatest and first commandment. And a second is like it: 'You shall love your neighbor as yourself.' On these two commandments hang all the law and the prophets."

Then a scribe said to him, "You are right, Teacher; you have truly said that 'he is one, and besides him there is no other'; and 'to love him with all the heart, and with all the understanding, and with all the strength,' and 'to love one's neighbor as oneself,' — this is much more important than all whole burnt offerings and sacrifices."

When Jesus saw that he answered wisely, he said to him, "You are not far from the kingdom of God."

Grant that we may love you tru - ly; Lord, our
thoughts and ac - tions sway, and to ev - 'ry heart more
ful - ly your a - ton - ing pow'r dis - play.

8.7.8.7. Trochaic
BATTY (16 A)

A Question about David's Son
Matthew 22:46; Mark 12:35-37

28 While Jesus was teaching in the temple, he said, "How can the scribes say that the Messiah is the son of David? David himself, by the Holy Spirit, declared, 'The Lord said to my Lord, Sit at my right hand, until I put your enemies under your

feet.' David himself calls him Lord; so how can he
be his son?"

No one was able to give him an answer, nor
from that day did anyone dare to ask him any more
questions. But the large crowd was listening to him
with delight.

1 Bliss be - yond com - pare, which in Christ I
2 Je - sus is my joy, there - fore blessed am

share! He's my on - ly joy and trea - sure;
I, O his mer - cy is un - bound - ed,

taste - less is all world - ly plea - sure, when in Christ I
all my hope on him is ground - ed; Je - sus is my

share bliss be - yond com - pare.
joy, there - fore blessed am I.

5.5.8.8.5.5. Trochaic
SEELENBRÄUTIGAM (68 A)

Woe to Scribes and Pharisees
Matthew 23:1-36

29 Then Jesus said to the crowds and to his disciples, "The scribes and the Pharisees sit on Moses' seat; therefore, do whatever they teach you and follow it; but do not do as they do, for they do not practice what they teach. They tie up heavy burdens, hard to bear, and lay them on the shoulders of others; but they themselves are unwilling to lift a finger to move them.

"They do all their deeds to be seen by others; for they make their phylacteries broad and their fringes long. They love to have the place of honor at banquets and the best seats in the synagogues, and to be greeted with respect in the marketplaces, and to have people call them rabbi.

"But you are not to be called rabbi, for you have one teacher, and you are all students. And call no one your father on earth, for you have one Father — the one in heaven. Nor are you to be called instructors, for you have one instructor, the Messiah. The greatest among you will be your servant. All who exalt themselves will be humbled, and all who humble themselves will be exalted."

30

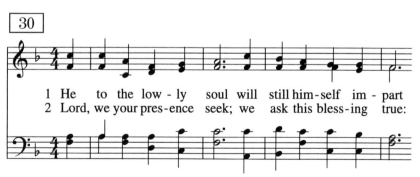

1 He   to the low - ly   soul will   still him-self im - part
2 Lord, we your pres-ence seek; we   ask this bless-ing true:

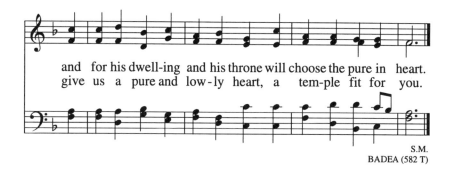

and for his dwell-ing and his throne will choose the pure in heart.
give us a pure and low-ly heart, a tem-ple fit for you.

S.M.
BADEA (582 T)

"But woe to you, scribes and Pharisees, hypocrites! For you lock people out of the kingdom of heaven. For you do not go in yourselves, and when others are going in, you stop them.

"Woe to you, scribes and Pharisees, hypocrites! For you cross sea and land to make a single convert, and you make the new convert twice as much a child of hell as yourselves.

"Woe to you, blind guides, who say, 'Whoever swears by the sanctuary is bound by nothing, but whoever swears by the gold of the sanctuary is bound by the oath.' You blind fools! For which is greater, the gold or the sanctuary that has made the gold sacred?

31 "And you say, 'Whoever swears by the altar is bound by nothing, but whoever swears by the gift that is on the altar is bound by the oath.' How blind you are! For which is greater, the gift or the altar that makes the gift sacred? So whoever swears by the altar, swears by it and by everything on it; and whoever swears by the sanctuary, swears by it and by the one who dwells in it; and whoever swears by

heaven, swears by the throne of God and by the one who is seated upon it.

"Woe to you, scribes and Pharisees, hypocrites! For you tithe mint, dill, and cummin, and have neglected the weightier matters of the law: justice and mercy and faith. It is these you ought to have practiced without neglecting the others. You blind guides! You strain out a gnat but swallow a camel!

"Woe to you, scribes and Pharisees, hypocrites! For you clean the outside of the cup and of the plate, but inside they are full of greed and self-indulgence. You blind Pharisee! First clean the inside of the cup, so that the outside also may become clean.

"Woe to you, scribes and Pharisees, hypocrites! For you are like whitewashed tombs, which on the outside look beautiful, but inside they are full of the bones of the dead and of all kinds of filth. So you also on the outside look righteous to others, but inside you are full of hypocrisy and lawlessness.

| 32 | "Woe to you, scribes and Pharisees, hypocrites! For you build the tombs of the prophets and decorate the graves of the righteous, and you say, 'If we had lived in the days of our ancestors, we would not have taken part with them in shedding the blood of the prophets.' Thus you testify against yourselves that you are descendants of those who murdered the prophets. Fill up, then, the measure of your ancestors.

"You snakes, you brood of vipers! How can

you escape being sentenced to hell? Therefore I send you prophets, sages, and scribes, some of whom you will kill and crucify, and some you will flog in your synagogues and pursue from town to town, so that upon you may come all the righteous blood shed on earth, from the blood of righteous Abel to the blood of Zechariah son of Barachiah, whom you murdered between the sanctuary and the altar. Truly I tell you, all this will come upon this generation."

Lament over Jerusalem
Matthew 23:37-39

"Jerusalem, Jerusalem, the city that kills the prophets and stones those who are sent to it! How often have I desired to gather your children together as a hen gathers her brood under her wings, and you were not willing! See, your house is left to you, desolate. For I tell you, you will not see me again until you say, 'Blessed is the one who comes in the name of the Lord.' "

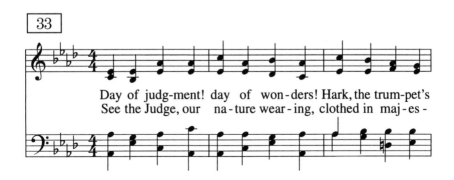

33

Day of judg-ment! day of won-ders! Hark, the trum-pet's
See the Judge, our na-ture wear-ing, clothed in maj-es-

aw - ful sound,   loud - er than a   thou - sand thun - ders,
ty di - vine;   all who love the Lord's ap - pear - ing

shakes the vast cre - a - tion round: how the sum - mons,
then shall say, "This God is mine." Gra - cious Sav - ior,

how the sum - mons will the sin - ner's heart con - found!
gra - cious Sav - ior, own me on that day as thine.

8.7.8.7.8 7 Trochaic
JUDGMENT (585 A)

The Widow's Offering
Mark 12:41-44

Jesus sat down opposite the treasury, and watched the crowd putting money into the treasury. Many rich people put in large sums. A poor widow came and put in two small copper coins, which are worth a penny.

Then he called his disciples and said to them, "Truly I tell you, this poor widow has put in more than all those who are contributing to the treasury.

For all of them have contributed out of their abundance; but she out of her poverty has put in everything she had, all she had to live on."

34

Je - sus, what of - f'ring shall I give to you, the Lord of earth and skies? My soul and bod - y now re - ceive, a ho - ly, liv - ing sac - ri - fice; small as it is, it's all my store; more should you have, if I had more.

8.8.8.8.8.8. Iambic
EISENACH (90 A)

The Unbelief of the People
John 12:36-43

After Jesus had said this, he departed and hid from them. Although he had performed so many signs in their presence, they did not believe in him. This was to fulfill the word spoken by the prophet Isaiah:

"Lord, who has believed our message, and to whom has the arm of the Lord been revealed?"

And so they could not believe, because Isaiah also said, "He has blinded their eyes and hardened their heart, so that they might not look with their eyes, and understand with their heart and turn — and I would heal them."

35 Isaiah said this because he saw his glory and spoke about him. Nevertheless many, even of the authorities, believed in Jesus. But because of the Pharisees they did not confess it, for fear that they would be put out of the synagogue; for they loved human glory more than the glory that comes from God.

If Christ is mine, let friends for-sake and earth-ly com-forts flee;

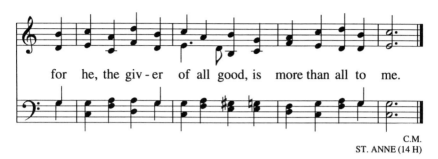

for he, the giv-er of all good, is more than all to me.

C.M.
ST. ANNE (14 H)

Summary of Jesus' Teaching
John 12:44-50

Then Jesus cried aloud: "Whoever believes in me believes not in me but in him who sent me. And whoever sees me sees him who sent me. I have come as light into the world, so that everyone who believes in me should not remain in the darkness. I do not judge anyone who hears my words and does not keep them, for I came not to judge the world, but to save the world. The one who rejects me and does not receive my word has a judge; on the last day the word that I have spoken will serve as judge, for I have not spoken on my own, but the Father who sent me has himself given me a commandment about what to say and what to speak. And I know that his commandment is eternal life. What I speak, therefore, I speak just as the Father has told me."

36

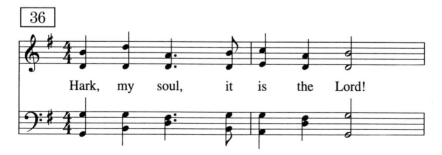

Hark, my soul, it is the Lord!

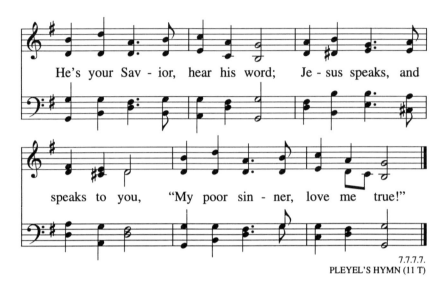

He's your Sav - ior, hear his word; Je - sus speaks, and

speaks to you, "My poor sin - ner, love me true!"

7.7.7.7.
PLEYEL'S HYMN (11 T)

Jesus Foretells the End of the Age and the Destruction of the Temple
Matthew 24:1-3

As Jesus came out of the temple and was going away, his disciples came to point out to him the buildings of the temple. Then he asked them, "You see all these, do you not? Truly I tell you, not one stone will be left here upon another; all will be thrown down."

When he was sitting on the Mount of Olives, the disciples came to him privately, saying, "Tell us, when will this be, and what will be the sign of your coming and of the end of the age?"

Signs of the End
Matthew 24:4-28; Luke 21:13-19

Jesus answered them, "Beware that no one leads you astray. For many will come in my name, saying, 'I am the Messiah!' and they will lead many astray. And you will hear of wars and rumors of wars; see that you are not alarmed; for this must take place, but the end is not yet. For nation will rise against nation, and kingdom against kingdom, and there will be famines and earthquakes in various places: all this is but the beginning of the birth pangs.

37 "Then they will hand you over to be tortured and will put you to death, and you will be hated by all nations because of my name.

"This will give you an opportunity to testify. So make up your minds not to prepare your defense in advance; for I will give you words and a wisdom that none of your opponents will be able to withstand or contradict. You will be betrayed even by parents and brothers, by relatives and friends; and they will put some of you to death. You will be hated by all because of my name. But not a hair of your head will perish. By your endurance you will gain your souls."

O teach us all your per - fect will to

un - der - stand and   to ful - fill: when hu - man in - sight

fails, give light; this   will di - rect our   steps a - right.

L.M.
HUS (22 F)

"Then many will fall away, and they will betray one another and hate one another. And many false prophets will arise and lead many astray. And because of the increase of lawlessness, the love of many will grow cold. But the one who endures to the end will be saved. And this good news of the kingdom will be proclaimed throughout the world, as a testimony to all the nations; and then the end will come."

38

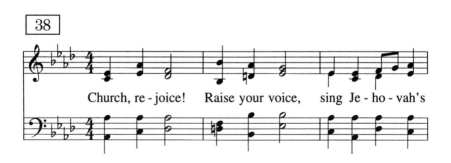

Church, re - joice! Raise your voice, sing Je - ho - vah's

wor - thy praise; ex - tol his name for - ev - er; laud
him, our God and Sav - ior; pro - claim to ev - 'ry
na - tion the ti - dings of sal - va - tion;
bear the wit - ness to his great - ness; spread the sto - ry
of his glo - ry to the earth's re - mot - est bounds.

3.3.7.7.7.7.7.4.4.4.4.7. Mixed
CHURCH, REJOICE! (225 A)

"So when you see the desolating sacrilege standing in the holy place, as was spoken of by the prophet Daniel, then those in Judea must flee to the mountains; the one on the housetop must not go down to take what is in the house; the one in the field must not turn back to get a coat.

"Woe to those who are pregnant and to those who are nursing infants in those days! Pray that your flight may not be in winter or on a sabbath. For at that time there will be great suffering, such as has not been from the beginning of the world until now, no, and never will be. And if those days had not been cut short, no one would be saved; but for the sake of the elect those days will be cut short.

[39] "Then if anyone says to you, 'Look! Here is the Messiah!' or 'There he is!' — do not believe it. For false messiahs and false prophets will appear and produce great signs and omens, to lead astray, if possible, even the elect. Take note, I have told you beforehand. So, if they say to you, 'Look! He is in the wilderness,' do not go out. If they say, 'Look! He is in the inner rooms,' do not believe it. For as the lightning comes from the east and flashes as far as the west, so will be the coming of the Son of Man. Wherever the corpse is, there the vultures will gather."

The Coming of the Son of Man
Matthew 24:29-33; Luke 21:28

"Immediately after the suffering of those days the sun will be darkened, and the moon will not give its light; the stars will fall from heaven, and the powers of heaven will be shaken. Then the sign of the Son of Man will appear in heaven, and then all the tribes of the earth will mourn, and they will see 'the Son of Man coming on the clouds of heaven' with power and great glory. And he will send out his angels with a loud trumpet call, and they will gather his elect from the four winds, from one end of heaven to the other.

"Now when these things begin to take place, stand up and raise your heads, because your redemption is drawing near."

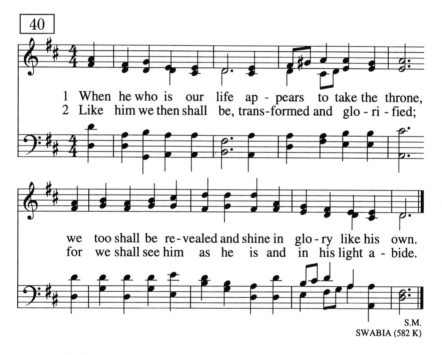

1 When he who is our life ap-pears to take the throne,
2 Like him we then shall be, trans-formed and glo-ri-fied;

we too shall be re-vealed and shine in glo-ry like his own.
for we shall see him as he is and in his light a-bide.

S.M.
SWABIA (582 K)

"From the fig tree learn its lesson: as soon as its branch becomes tender and puts forth its leaves, you know that summer is near. So also, when you see all these things, you know that he is near, at the very gates."

The Need for Watchfulness
Matthew 24:36-44; Mark 13:34-37

"But about that day and hour no one knows, neither the angels of heaven, nor the Son, but only the Father. For as the days of Noah were, so will be the coming of the Son of Man. For as in those days before the flood they were eating and drinking, marrying and giving in marriage, until the day Noah entered the ark, and they knew nothing until the flood came and swept them all away, so too will be the coming of the Son of Man.

41 "Then two will be in the field; one will be taken and one will be left. Two women will be grinding meal together; one will be taken and one will be left. Keep awake therefore, for you do not know on what day your Lord is coming."

Lord, for your com-ing us pre-pare; may we, to meet you with-out fear, at all times read-y be; in

faith and love pre - serve us sound; O let us day and

night be found wait - ing with joy your face to see.

7.7.6.7.7.8.
INNSBRUCK (79 A)

"It is like a man going on a journey, when he leaves home and puts his slaves in charge, each with his work, and commands the doorkeeper to be on the watch. Therefore, keep awake — for you do not know when the master of the house will come, in the evening, or at midnight, or at cockcrow, or at dawn, or else he may find you asleep when he comes suddenly. And what I say to you I say to all: Keep awake."

You ser-vants of the Lord, each in your of - fice wait,

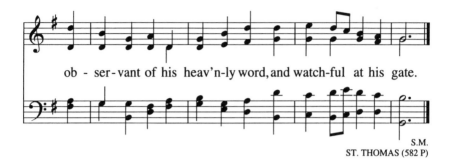

ob - ser-vant of his heav'n-ly word, and watch-ful at his gate.

S.M.
ST. THOMAS (582 P)

42 "But understand this: if the owner of the house had known in what part of the night the thief was coming, he would have stayed awake and would not have let his house be broken into. Therefore you also must be ready, for the Son of Man is coming at an unexpected hour."

The Faithful/Unfaithful Slave
Matthew 24:45-51

"Who then is the faithful and wise slave, whom his master has put in charge of his household, to give the other slaves their allowance of food at the proper time? Blessed is that slave whom his master will find at work when he arrives. Truly I tell you, he will put that one in charge of all his possessions. But if that wicked slave says to himself, 'My master is delayed,' and he begins to beat his fellow slaves, and eats and drinks with drunkards, the master of that slave will come on a day when he does not expect him and at an hour that he does not know. He will cut him in pieces and put him with the hypocrites, where there will be weeping and gnashing of teeth."

O bless - ed hope! In faith we wait,

hear-ing his foot - steps at the gate, while we his

tri - umph cel - e - brate un - til he comes.

Margaret Clarkson. © Hope Publishing Company. Used by permission.

8.8.8.4. Iambic
ALMSGIVING (3 C)

Parable of the Wise and Foolish Bridesmaids
Matthew 25:1-13

43 "Then the kingdom of heaven will be like this. Ten bridesmaids took their lamps and went to meet the bridegroom. Five of them were foolish, and five were wise. When the foolish took their lamps, they took no oil with them; but the wise took flasks of oil with their lamps. As the bridegroom was delayed, all of them became drowsy and slept. But at midnight there was a shout, 'Look! Here is the bridegroom! Come out to meet him.' "

Re-joice, re-joice, be-liev-ers, and let your lights ap-pear;

the eve-ning is ad-vanc-ing, and dark-er night is near.

The bride-groom is a-ris-ing and soon is draw-ing nigh.

Up, pray and watch and wres-tle; at mid-night comes the cry.

7.6.7.6.D. Iambic
REJOICE (151 I)

"Then all those bridesmaids got up and trimmed their lamps. The foolish said to the wise, 'Give us some of your oil, for our lamps are going out.' But the wise replied, 'No! there will not be enough for you and for us; you had better go to the dealers and buy some for yourselves.'

44 "And while they went to buy it, the bridegroom came, and those who were ready went with him into the wedding banquet; and the door was shut. Later the other bridesmaids came also, saying, 'Lord, lord, open to us.' But he replied, 'Truly I tell you, I do not know you.' Keep awake therefore, for you know neither the day nor the hour."

7.6.7.6.D. Iambic
REJOICE (151 I)

Parable of the Talents
Matthew 25:14-30

"For it is as if a man, going on a journey, summoned his slaves and entrusted his property to them; to one he gave five talents, to another two, to another one, to each according to his ability. Then he went away.

"The one who had received the five talents went off at once and traded with them, and made five more talents. In the same way, the one who had the two talents made two more talents. But the one who had received the one talent went off and dug a hole in the ground and hid his master's money.

 45 "After a long time the master of those slaves came and settled accounts with them. Then the one who had received the five talents came forward, bringing five more talents, saying, 'Master, you handed over to me five talents; see, I have made five more talents.' His master said to him, 'Well done, good and trustworthy slave; you have been trustworthy in a few things, I will put you in charge of many things; enter into the joy of your master.'

"And the one with the two talents also came forward, saying, 'Master, you handed over to me two talents; see, I have made two more talents.' His master said to him, 'Well done, good and trustworthy slave; you have been trustworthy in a few things, I will put you in charge of many things; enter into the joy of your master.'

"Then the one who had received the one talent also came forward, saying, 'Master, I knew that you were a harsh man, reaping where you did not sow, and gathering where you did not scatter seed; so I was afraid, and I went and hid your talent in the ground. Here you have what is yours.' But his master replied, 'You wicked and lazy slave! You knew, did you, that I reap where I did not sow, and gather where I did not scatter? Then you ought to have invested my money with the bankers, and on my return I would have received what was my own with interest. So take the talent from him, and give it to the one with the ten talents.

46   For to all those who have, more will be given, and they will have an abundance; but from those who have nothing, even what they have will be taken away. As for this worthless slave, throw him into the outer darkness, where there will be weeping and gnashing of teeth.'"

Help us, O God, to use our gifts in ser-vice day by day,

that what you give us we may share, and work as well as pray.

C.M.
ST. ANNE (14 H)

The Great Judgment
Matthew 25:31-46

"When the Son of Man comes in his glory, and all the angels with him, then he will sit on the throne of his glory. All the nations will be gathered before him, and he will separate people one from another as a shepherd separates the sheep from the goats, and he will put the sheep at his right hand and the goats at the left.

"Then the king will say to those at his right hand, 'Come, you that are blessed by my Father, inherit the kingdom prepared for you from the foundation of the world; for I was hungry and you gave me food, I was thirsty and you gave me something to drink, I was a stranger and you welcomed me, I was naked and you gave me clothing, I was sick and you took care of me, I was in prison and you visited me.'

47 "Then the righteous will answer him, 'Lord, when was it that we saw you hungry and gave you food, or thirsty and gave you something to drink? And when was it that we saw you a stranger and welcomed you, or naked and gave you clothing? And when was it that we saw you sick or in prison and visited you?' And the king will answer them, 'Truly I tell you, just as you did it to one of the least of these who are members of my family, you did it to me.'

"Then he will say to those at his left hand, 'You that are accursed, depart from me into the eternal fire prepared for the devil and his angels; for I was hungry and you gave me no food, I was thirsty and you gave me nothing to drink, I was a stranger and you did not welcome me, naked and you did not give me clothing, sick and in prison and you did not visit me.'

  "Then they also will answer, 'Lord, when was it that we saw you hungry or thirsty or a stranger or naked or sick or in prison, and did not take care of you?' Then he will answer them, 'Truly I tell you, just as you did not do it to one of the least of these, you did not do it to me.' And these will go away into eternal punishment, but the righteous into eternal life."

48

1 Where cross the crowd-ed ways of life, where sound the
2 The cup of wa-ter giv'n for you still holds the

cries of race and clan, a-bove the noise of
fresh-ness of your grace, yet long these mul-ti-

self-ish strife we hear your voice, O Son of Man.
tudes to view the strong com-pas-sion in your face.

L.M.
GERMANY (22 R)

The Plot to Kill Jesus
Matthew 26:1-2; Mark 14:1-2; Luke 22:3-6

When Jesus had finished saying all these things, he said to his disciples, "You know that after two days the Passover is coming, and the Son of Man will be handed over to be crucified."

The chief priests and the scribes were looking for a way to arrest Jesus by stealth and kill him; for they said, "Not during the festival, or there may be a riot among the people."

Then Satan entered into Judas called Iscariot, who was one of the twelve; he went away and conferred with the chief priests and officers of the temple police about how he might betray him to them. They were greatly pleased and agreed to give him money. So he consented and began to look for an opportunity to betray him to them when no crowd was present.

49

O Lamb of God, still keep me near to your wound-ed side;

'tis on-ly there in safe-ty and peace I can a-bide!

What foes and snares sur-round me! What doubts and fears with-in!

The grace that sought and found me a-lone can keep me clean.

7.6.7.6.D.
ST. EDITH (151 Q)

(For Wednesday and most of Thursday nothing has been recorded. It would appear Jesus remained with his disciples at Bethany.)

Thursday Evening

Preparation for the Passover
Luke 22:7-13; John 13:1

50 Then came the day of Unleavened Bread, on which the Passover lamb had to be sacrificed. So Jesus sent Peter and John, saying, "Go and prepare the Passover meal for us that we may eat it."

They asked him, "Where do you want us to make preparations for it?"

"Listen," he said to them, "when you have entered the city, a man carrying a jar of water will meet you; follow him into the house he enters and say to the owner of the house, 'The teacher asks you, "Where is the guest room, where I may eat the Passover with my disciples?"' He will show you a large room upstairs, already furnished. Make preparations for us there." So they went and found everything as he had told them; and they prepared the Passover meal.

Now before the festival of the Passover, Jesus knew that his hour had come to depart from this world and go to the Father. Having loved his own who were in the world, he loved them to the end.

"Mine is an un-chang-ing love,
high-er than the heights a-bove, deep-er than the
depths be-neath, free and faith-ful, strong as death."

7.7.7.7. Trochaic
ST. BEES (11 U)

The Last Supper
Luke 22:14-17, 24-27

When the hour came, he took his place at the table, and the apostles with him. He said to them, "I have eagerly desired to eat this Passover with you before I suffer; for I tell you, I will not eat it until it is fulfilled in the kingdom of God."

A dispute also arose among them as to which one of them was to be regarded as the greatest. But he said to them, "The kings of the Gentiles lord it over them; and those in authority over them are called benefactors. But not so with you; rather the greatest among you must become like the youngest, and the leader like one who serves. For who is greater, the one who is at the table or the one who serves? Is it not the one at the table? But I am among you as one who serves."

Jesus Washes the Disciples' Feet
John 13:2-20

[52] During supper Jesus, knowing that the Father had given all things into his hands, and that he had come from God and was going to God, got up from the table, took off his outer robe, and tied a towel around himself. Then he poured water into a basin and began to wash the disciples' feet and to wipe them with the towel that was tied around him. He came to Simon Peter, who said to him, "Lord, are you going to wash my feet?"

Jesus answered, "You do not know now what I am doing, but later you will understand."

Peter said to him, "You will never wash my feet." Jesus answered, "Unless I wash you, you have no share with me."

Simon Peter said to him, "Lord, not my feet only but also my hands and my head!"

Jesus said to him, "One who has bathed does not need to wash, except for the feet, but is entirely clean. And you are clean, though not all of you." For he knew who was to betray him; for this reason he said, "Not all of you are clean."

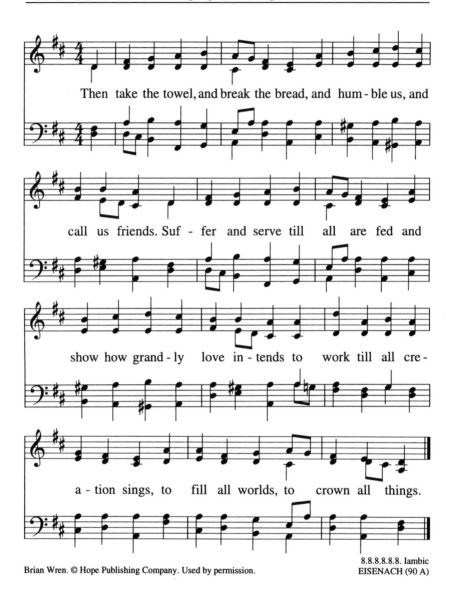

Then take the towel, and break the bread, and hum - ble us, and

call us friends. Suf - fer and serve till all are fed and

show how grand - ly love in - tends to work till all cre -

a - tion sings, to fill all worlds, to crown all things.

Brian Wren. © Hope Publishing Company. Used by permission.

8.8.8.8.8.8. Iambic
EISENACH (90 A)

53 After he had washed their feet, had put on his robe, and had returned to the table, he said to them, "Do you know what I have done to you? You call me Teacher and Lord — and you are right, for that is

what I am. So if I, your Lord and Teacher, have washed your feet, you also ought to wash one another's feet. For I have set you an example, that you also should do as I have done to you.

"Very truly, I tell you, servants are not greater than their master, nor are messengers greater than the one who sent them. If you know these things, you are blessed if you do them.

"I am not speaking of all of you; I know whom I have chosen. But it is to fulfill the scripture, 'The one who ate my bread has lifted his heel against me.' I tell you this now, before it occurs, so that when it does occur, you may believe that I am he. Very truly, I tell you, whoever receives one whom I send receives me; and whoever receives me receives him who sent me."

Bless - ed Je - sus, at your word we are gath - ered all to hear you; let our hearts and souls be stirred

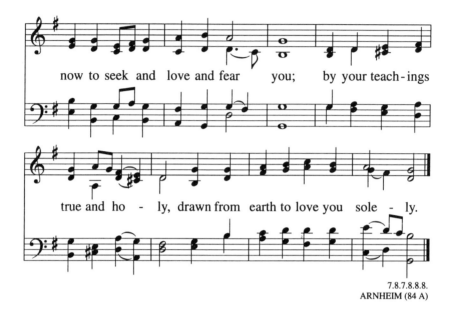

now to seek and love and fear you; by your teach-ings

true and ho - ly, drawn from earth to love you sole - ly.

7.8.7.8.8.8.
ARNHEIM (84 A)

Jesus Foretells His Betrayer
Mark 14:18-21; John 13:22-31

54 As they were eating, Jesus said, "Truly I tell you, one of you will betray me, one who is eating with me."

They began to be distressed and to say to him one after another, "Surely, not I?"

He said to them, "It is one of the twelve, one who is dipping bread into the bowl with me. For the Son of Man goes as it is written of him, but woe to that one by whom the Son of Man is betrayed! It would have been better for that one not to have been born."

The disciples looked at one another, uncertain of whom he was speaking. One of his disciples — the one whom Jesus loved — was reclining next to him; Simon Peter therefore motioned to him to ask Jesus of whom he was speaking.

So while reclining next to Jesus, he asked him, "Lord, who is it?"

Jesus answered, "It is the one to whom I give this piece of bread when I have dipped it in the dish." So when he had dipped the piece of bread, he gave it to Judas son of Simon Iscariot. After he received the piece of bread, Satan entered into him. Jesus said to him, "Do quickly what you are going to do."

55 Now no one at the table knew why he said this to him. Some thought that, because Judas had the common purse, Jesus was telling him, "Buy what we need for the festival"; or, that he should give something to the poor. So, after receiving the piece of bread, he immediately went out. And it was night.

Je - sus, price-less trea - sure, source of pur - est plea - sure,

friend to me so true, how my heart has pant - ed and my soul has

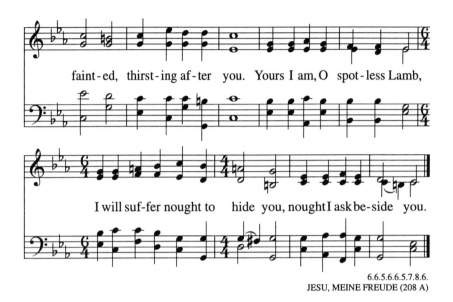

faint-ed, thirst-ing af-ter you. Yours I am, O spot-less Lamb,

I will suf-fer nought to hide you, nought I ask be-side you.

6.6.5.6.6.5.7.8.6.
JESU, MEINE FREUDE (208 A)

When he had gone out, Jesus said, "Now the Son of Man has been glorified, and God has been glorified in him."

(Standing)

Institution of the Lord's Supper
Mark 14:22-25

56 While they were eating, he took a loaf of bread, and after blessing it he broke it, gave it to them, and said, "Take; this is my body." Then he took a cup, and after giving thanks he gave it to them, and all of them drank from it. He said to them, "This is my blood of the covenant, which is poured out for many. Truly I tell you, I will never again drink of the fruit of the vine until that day when I drink it new in the kingdom of God."

(Sitting or kneeling)

Silent Prayer

*(During the silent prayer,
the choir may sing:)*

O what an act of maj-es-ty! O what a love be-

yond de-gree! O what a hal-lowed hour of bless - ing!

Here soul and bod-y are sup-plied, and we show forth that

Je-sus died, when in this feast our Lord con-fess - ing.

8.8.9.8.8.9.
O ANBLICK (99 B)

By all the merits of your life,
By your humility, meekness, and patience,
By your griefs and sorrows,
By your prayers and tears,
By your having been despised and rejected,
By your atoning death,
By your divine presence,
By the holy sacraments,
Bless and comfort us, gracious Lord
and God.

(Sitting)

See, the feast of love is spread, drink the wine and break the bread— sweet me - mo - rials— till the Lord call us round his heav'n - ly board; some from earth, from

glo - ry some,   sev - ered on - ly "Till he come!"

7.7.7.7.7.7.
WELLS

The New Commandment
John 13:33-35

"Little children, I am with you only a little longer. You will look for me; and as I said to the Jews so now I say to you, 'Where I am going, you cannot come.' I give you a new commandment, that you love one another. Just as I have loved you, you also should love one another. By this everyone will know that you are my disciples, if you have love for one another."

Jesus Foretells Peter's Denial
Matthew 26:35; Luke 22:31-33;
John 13:36-38

Simon Peter said to him, "Lord, where are you going?"

Jesus answered, "Where I am going, you cannot follow me now; but you will follow afterward."

Peter said to him, "Lord, why can I not follow you now? I will lay down my life for you."

[58] Jesus answered, "Will you lay down your life for me? Very truly, I tell you, before the cock crows, you will have denied me three times."

Peter said to him, "Even though I must die with you, I will not deny you." And so said all the disciples.

Jesus responded, "Simon, Simon, listen! Satan has demanded to sift all of you like wheat, but I have prayed for you that your own faith may not fail; and you, when once you have turned back, strengthen your brothers."

More love to thee, O Christ! More love to thee;

hear thou the prayer I make on bend-ed knee;

this is my ear-nest plea, more love, O Christ, to thee,

more love to thee, more love to thee!

6.4.6.4.6.6.4.4.
DEVOTION

Purse, Bag, and Sword
Luke 22:35-38

Jesus said to them, "When I sent you out without a purse, bag, or sandals, did you lack anything?"

They said, "No, not a thing."

59 He said to them, "But now, the one who has a purse must take it, and likewise a bag. And the one who has no sword must sell his cloak and buy one. For I tell you, this scripture must be fulfilled in me, 'And he was counted among the lawless'; and indeed what is written about me is being fulfilled."

They said, "Lord, look, here are two swords."

He replied, "It is enough."

It is e-nough: earth's strug-gles soon shall cease
and Je-sus call us to heav'n's per - fect peace.

10.10. Iambic
COENA DOMINI (1 C)

Jesus Is the Way to the Father
John 14:1-14

Jesus continued, "Do not let your hearts be troubled. Believe in God, believe also in me. In my Father's house there are many dwelling places. If it were not so, would I have told you that I go to prepare a place for you? And if I go and prepare a place for you, I will come again and will take you to myself, so that where I am, there you may be also. And you know the way to the place where I am going."

1 You are the way; to you a-lone from sin and death we flee;
2 You are the way, the truth, the life; grant us that way to know,

and those who would the Fa-ther seek your fol-low-ers must be.
that truth to keep, that life to win, whose joys e-ter-nal flow.

C.M.
DUNDEE (14 P)

Thomas said to Jesus, "Lord, we do not know where we are going. How can we know the way?" Jesus said to him, "I am the way, and the truth, and the life. No one comes to the Father except through me. If you know me, you will know my Father also. From now on you do know him and have seen him."

Philip said to him, "Lord, show us the Father, and we will be satisfied."

Jesus said to him, "Have I been with you all this time, Philip, and you still do not know me? Whoever has seen me has seen the Father. How can you say, 'Show us the Father'? Do you not believe that I am in the Father and the Father is in me? The words that I say to you I do not speak on my own; but the Father who dwells in me does his works. Believe me that I am in the Father and the Father is in me; but if you do not, then believe me because of the works themselves.

61 "Very truly, I tell you, the one who believes in me will also do the works that I do and, in fact, will do greater works than these, because I am going to the Father. I will do whatever you ask in my name, so that the Father may be glorified in the Son. If in my name you ask me for anything, I will do it."

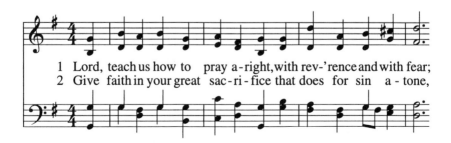

1 Lord, teach us how to pray a-right, with rev-'rence and with fear;
2 Give faith in your great sac-ri-fice that does for sin a-tone,

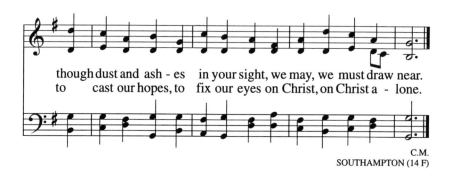

though dust and ash - es   in your sight, we may, we must draw near.
to   cast our hopes, to   fix our eyes on Christ, on Christ a - lone.

C.M.
SOUTHAMPTON (14 F)

The Promise of the Holy Spirit
John 14:15-31

"If you love me, you will keep my commandments. And I will ask the Father, and he will give you another Advocate, to be with you forever. This is the Spirit of truth, whom the world cannot receive, because it neither sees him nor knows him. You know him, because he abides with you, and he will be in you.

62 "I will not leave you orphaned; I am coming to you. In a little while the world will no longer see me, but you will see me; because I live, you also will live. On that day you will know that I am in my Father, and you in me, and I in you. They who have my commandments and keep them are those who love me; and those who love me will be loved by my Father, and I will love them and reveal myself to them."

Judas (not Iscariot) said to him, "Lord, how is it that you will reveal yourself to us, and not to the world?"

Jesus answered him, "Those who love me will keep my word, and my Father will love them, and we will come to them and make our home with them. Whoever does not love me does not keep my words; and the word that you hear is not mine, but is from the Father who sent me.

"I have said these things to you while I am still with you. But the Advocate, the Holy Spirit, whom the Father will send in my name, will teach you everything, and remind you of all that I have said to you.

"Peace I leave with you; my peace I give to you. I do not give to you as the world gives. Do not let your hearts be troubled, and do not let them be afraid.

63 "You heard me say to you, 'I am going away, and I am coming to you.' If you loved me, you would rejoice that I am going to the Father, because the Father is greater than I. And now I have told you this before it occurs, so that when it does occur, you may believe.

"I will no longer talk much with you, for the ruler of this world is coming. He has no power over me; but I do as the Father has commanded me, so that the world may know that I love the Father."

Christ is our Mas-ter, Lord, and God, the full-ness of the

Three in One. His life, death, right-eous-ness, and blood our

faith's foun-da-tion are a-lone; his God-head and his

death shall be our theme to all e-ter-ni-ty.

8.8.8.8.8.8. Iambic
EISENACH (90 A)

Jesus the True Vine
John 15:1-17

When they had sung a hymn, Jesus said, "I am the true vine, and my Father is the vinegrower. He removes every branch in me that bears no fruit. Every branch that bears fruit he prunes to make it bear more fruit.

64 "You have already been cleansed by the word that I have spoken to you. Abide in me as I abide in you. Just as the branch cannot bear fruit by itself unless it abides in the vine, neither can you unless

you abide in me. I am the vine, you are the branches. Those who abide in me and I in them bear much
fruit, because apart from me you can do nothing.
Whoever does not abide in me is thrown away like
a branch and withers; such branches are gathered,
thrown into the fire, and burned. If you abide in me,
and my words abide in you, ask for whatever you
wish, and it will be done for you. My Father is glorified by this, that you bear much fruit and become
my disciples. As the Father has loved me, so I have
loved you; abide in my love. If you keep my commandments, you will abide in my love, just as I
have kept my Father's commandments and abide in
his love."

You are the vine; your heav'n - ly root sup -
plies each branch with life and fruit; O may a last - ing
un - ion join my soul to Christ, the liv - ing vine!

L.M.
TALLIS' CANON (22 T)

"I have said these things to you so that my joy may be in you, and that your joy may be complete.

"This is my commandment, that you love one another as I have loved you. No one has greater love than this, to lay down one's life for one's friends. You are my friends if you do what I command you.

"I do not call you servants any longer, because the servant does not know what the master is doing; but I have called you friends, because I have made known to you everything that I have heard from my Father.

⬚ 65 ⬚ "You did not choose me but I chose you. And I appointed you to go and bear fruit, fruit that will last, so that the Father will give you whatever you ask him in my name. I am giving you these commands so that you may love one another."

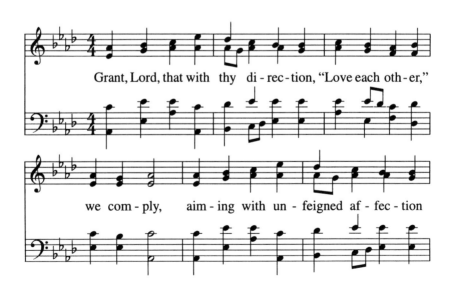

Grant, Lord, that with thy di - rec - tion, "Love each oth - er,"

we com - ply,   aim - ing with un - feigned af - fec - tion

thy love to ex - em - pli - fy; let our mu - tual love be glow - ing;

thus the world will plain - ly see that we, as on

one stem grow - ing, liv - ing branch - es are in thee.

8.7.8.7.D. Trochaic
CASSEL (167 A)

The World's Hatred
John 15:18-16:4

"If the world hates you, be aware that it hated me before it hated you. If you belonged to the world, the world would love you as its own. Because you do not belong to the world, but I have chosen you out of the world — therefore the world hates you.

"Remember the word that I said to you, 'Servants are not greater than their master.' If they persecuted me, they will persecute you; if they kept my word, they will keep yours also.

66 But they will do all these things to you on account of my name, because they do not know him who sent me.

"If I had not come and spoken to them, they would not have sin; but now they have no excuse for their sin. Whoever hates me hates my Father also.

"If I had not done among them the works that no one else did, they would not have sin. But now they have seen and hated both me and my Father. It was to fulfill the word that is written in their law, 'They hated me without a cause.'

"When the Advocate comes, whom I will send to you from the Father, the Spirit of truth who comes from the Father, he will testify on my behalf. You also are to testify because you have been with me from the beginning."

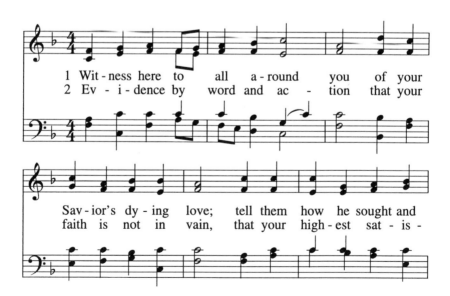

1 Wit-ness here to all a-round you of your
2 Ev-i-dence by word and ac - tion that your

Sav-ior's dy-ing love; tell them how he sought and
faith is not in vain, that your high-est sat-is-

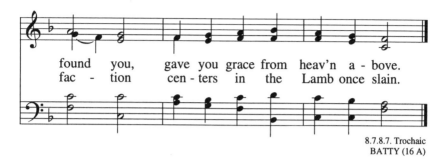

found you, gave you grace from heav'n a - bove.
fac - tion cen - ters in the Lamb once slain.

8.7.8.7. Trochaic
BATTY (16 A)

67 "I have said these things to you to keep you from stumbling. They will put you out of the synagogues. Indeed, an hour is coming when those who kill you will think that by doing so they are offering worship to God. And they will do this because they have not known the Father or me. But I have said these things to you so that when their hour comes you may remember that I told you about them."

The Work of the Spirit
John 16:4-15

"I did not say these things to you from the beginning, because I was with you. But now I am going to him who sent me; yet none of you asks me, 'Where are you going?' But because I have said these things to you, sorrow has filled your hearts.

"Nevertheless I tell you the truth: it is to your advantage that I go away, for if I do not go away, the Advocate will not come to you; but if I go, I will send him to you. And when he comes, he will prove the world wrong about sin and righteousness and judgment: about sin, because they do not believe in me; about righteousness, because I am going to the Father and you will see me no longer; about judgment, because the ruler of this world has been condemned."

Most ten-der Spir-it, might-y God, sweet must thy pres-ence be,

if loss of Je-sus can be gain, so long as we have thee.

C.M.
DUNDEE (14 P)

"I still have many things to say to you, but you cannot bear them now. When the Spirit of truth comes, he will guide you into all the truth; for he will not speak on his own, but will speak whatever he hears, and he will declare to you the things that are to come. He will glorify me, because he will take what is mine and declare it to you. All that the Father has is mine. For this reason I said that he will take what is mine and declare it to you."

Sorrow Will Turn to Joy
John 16:16-33

"A little while, and you will no longer see me, and again a little while, and you will see me."

Then some of his disciples said to one another, "What does he mean by saying to us, 'A little while, and you will no longer see me, and again a little while, and you will see me'; and 'Because I am going to the Father'?" They said, "What does he mean by this 'a little while'? We do not know what he is talking about."

69 Jesus knew that they wanted to ask him, so he said to them, "Are you discussing among yourselves what I meant when I said, 'A little while, and you will no longer see me, and again a little while, and you will see me'? Very truly, I tell you, you will weep and mourn, but the world will rejoice; you will have pain, but your pain will turn into joy. When a woman is in labor, she has pain, because her hour has come. But when her child is born, she no longer remembers the anguish because of the joy of having brought a human being into the world. So you have pain now; but I will see you again, and your hearts will rejoice, and no one will take your joy from you. On that day you will ask nothing of me. Very truly, I tell you, if you ask anything of the Father in my name, he will give it to you. Until now you have not asked for anything in my name. Ask and you will receive, so that your joy may be complete."

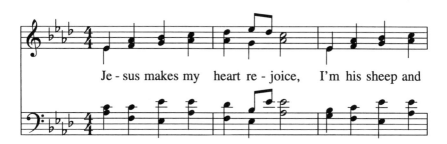

Je - sus makes my heart re - joice, I'm his sheep and

know his voice; he's a Shep-herd, kind and gra-cious,

and his pas-tures are de - li-cious; con-stant love to

me he shows, yea, my ver - y name he knows.

7.7.8.8.7.7. Trochaic
HAYN (82 D)

70 "I have said these things to you in figures of speech. The hour is coming when I will no longer speak to you in figures, but will tell you plainly of the Father. On that day you will ask in my name. I do not say to you that I will ask the Father on your behalf; for the Father himself loves you, because you have loved me and have believed that I came from God. I came from the Father and have come into the world; again, I am leaving the world and am going to the Father."

His disciples said, "Yes, now you are speaking plainly, not in any figure of speech! Now we know that you know all things, and do not need to have anyone question you; by this we believe that you came from God."

Jesus answered them, "Do you now believe? The hour is coming, indeed it has come, when you will be scattered, each one to his home, and you will leave me alone. Yet I am not alone because the Father is with me. I have said this to you, so that in me you may have peace. In the world you face persecution. But take courage; I have conquered the world!"

1 Je - sus, still lead on till our rest be won; and al - though the way be cheer - less, we will fol - low, calm and fear - less; guide us by your

2 Je - sus, still lead on till our rest be won; heav'n-ly lead - er, still di - rect us, still sup-port, con - sole, pro-tect us, till we safe - ly

hand   to the prom - ised   land.
stand   in the prom - ised   land.

5.5.8.8.5.5. Trochaic
SEELENBRÄUTIGAM (68 A)

(Standing)

Jesus Prays for His Disciples
John 17:1-26

After Jesus had spoken these words, he looked up to heaven and said, "Father, the hour has come; glorify your Son so that the Son may glorify you, since you have given him authority over all people, to give eternal life to all whom you have given him. And this is eternal life, that they may know you, the only true God, and Jesus Christ whom you have sent.

"I glorified you on earth by finishing the work that you gave me to do. So now, Father, glorify me in your own presence with the glory that I had in your presence before the world existed.

72 "I have made your name known to those whom you gave me from the world. They were yours, and you gave them to me, and they have kept your word. Now they know that everything you have given me is from you; for the words that you gave to me I have given to them, and they have

received them and know in truth that I came from you; and they have believed that you sent me.

"I am asking on their behalf; I am not asking on behalf of the world, but on behalf of those whom you gave me, because they are yours. All mine are yours, and yours are mine; and I have been glorified in them. And now I am no longer in the world, but they are in the world, and I am coming to you. Holy Father, protect them in your name that you have given me, so that they may be one, as we are one.

"While I was with them, I protected them in your name that you have given me. I guarded them, and not one of them was lost except the one destined to be lost, so that the scripture might be fulfilled. But now I am coming to you, and I speak these things in the world so that they may have my joy made complete in themselves.

| 73 | "I have given them your word, and the world has hated them because they do not belong to the world, just as I do not belong to the world. I am not asking you to take them out of the world, but I ask you to protect them from the evil one. They do not belong to the world, just as I do not belong to the world. Sanctify them in the truth; your word is truth.

"As you have sent me into the world, so I have sent them into the world. And for their sakes I sanctify myself, so that they also may be sanctified in truth.

"I ask not only on behalf of these, but also on behalf of those who will believe in me through their word, that they may all be one. As you, Father, are in me and I am in you, may they also be in us, so that the world may believe that you have sent me. The glory that you have given me I have given them, so that they may be one, as we are one, I in them and you in me, that they may become completely one, so that the world may know that you have sent me and have loved them even as you have loved me.

"Father, I desire that those also, whom you have given me, may be with me where I am, to see my glory, which you have given me because you loved me before the foundation of the world.

"Righteous Father, the world does not know you, but I know you; and these know that you have sent me. I made your name known to them, and I will make it known, so that the love with which you have loved me may be in them, and I in them."

74

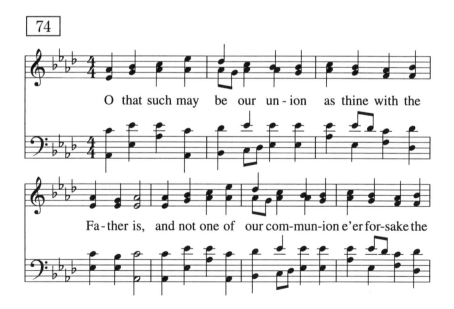

O that such may be our un - ion as thine with the

Fa - ther is, and not one of our com-mun-ion e'er for-sake the

path of bliss;   may our light break forth with bright-ness,

from thy light re - flect - ed shine;   thus the world will

bear us wit - ness that we, Lord, are   tru - ly thine.

8.7.8.7.D. Trochaic
CASSEL (167 A)

(Sitting)

The Agony in Gethsemane
John 18:1-2; Matthew 26:36-39;
Luke 22:43-44

After Jesus had spoken these words, he went out with his disciples across the Kidron valley to a place where there was a garden called Gethsemane, which he and his disciples entered. Now Judas, who betrayed him, also knew the place, because Jesus often met there with his disciples.

'Tis mid-night and on Ol-ive's brow the
star is dimmed that late-ly shone; 'tis mid-night; in the
gar-den now the suf-f'ring Sav-ior prays a-lone.

L.M.
OLIVE'S BROW

75 Then he said to his disciples, "Sit here while I go over there and pray." He took with him Peter and the two sons of Zebedee and said to them, "I am deeply grieved, even to death; remain here, and stay awake with me." And going a little farther, he threw himself on the ground and prayed, "My Father, if it is possible, let this cup pass from me; yet not what I want but what you want."

In the last hour of deep dis-tress, be-fore his Fa-ther's throne, with soul re-signed, he bowed and said, "Thy will, not mine, be done!"

C.M.
BEDFORD (14 C)

Then an angel from heaven appeared to him and gave him strength.

∾

(Standing)

In his anguish he prayed more earnestly, and his sweat became like great drops of blood falling down on the ground.

∾

(Sitting or kneeling)

Silent Prayer

*(During the silent prayer,
the choir may sing:)*

76

O there's a sight that rends my heart, nor can it from my
mind de - part, how you on Ol - i - vet did lan - guish;
O Lord, for your soul's ag - o - ny, when wrest - ling there with
death for me, make me a tro - phy of your an - guish.

8.8.9.8.8.9. Iambic
O ANBLICK (99 B)

(Or the congregation may sing:)

Go to dark Geth-sem-a-ne, all who feel the tempt-er's pow'r;

your Re-deem-er's con-flict see, watch with him one bit-ter hour.

Turn not from his griefs a-way; learn of Je-sus Christ to pray.

7.7.7.7.7.7. Trochaic
LATROBE (581 A)

By your prayers and tears,
By all the troubles of your life,
By the grief and anguish of your soul,
By your agony and bloody sweat,
Bless and comfort us, gracious Lord
and God.

(Sitting)

Betrayal and Arrest of Jesus
Matthew 26:40-56; Mark 14:44-46, 51-52;
John 18:3-9

77 Then he came to the disciples and found them sleeping; and he said to Peter, "So, could you not stay awake with me one hour? Stay awake and pray that you may not come into the time of trial; the spirit indeed is willing, but the flesh is weak."

Again he went away for the second time and prayed, "My Father, if this cannot pass unless I drink it, your will be done."

Again he came and found them sleeping, for their eyes were heavy. So leaving them again, he went away and prayed for the third time, saying the same words.

Then he came to the disciples and said to them, "Are you still sleeping and taking your rest? See, the hour is at hand, and the Son of Man is betrayed into the hands of sinners. Get up, let us be going. See, my betrayer is at hand."

While he was still speaking, Judas brought a detachment of soldiers together with police from the chief priests and the Pharisees, and they came there with lanterns and torches and weapons. Then Jesus, knowing all that was to happen to him, came forward and asked them, "Whom are you looking for?"

They answered, "Jesus of Nazareth."

Jesus replied, "I am he."

78 Judas, who betrayed him, was standing with them. When Jesus said to them, "I am he," they stepped back and fell to the ground.

Again he asked them, "Whom are you looking for?"

And they said, "Jesus of Nazareth."

Jesus answered, "I told you that I am he. So if you are looking for me, let these men go." This was to fulfill the word that he had spoken, "I did not lose a single one of those whom you gave me."

Now the betrayer had given them a sign, saying, "The one I will kiss is the man; arrest him and lead him away under guard." So when he came, he went up to him at once and said, "Rabbi!" and kissed him. Then they laid hands on him and arrested him.

My Sav-ior was be-tray-ed, re-proach and pain to meet;

my sins the Lord con-vey-ed 'fore Pi-late's judg-ment seat;

these, these did him de-liv-er in-to the foe's dire hand;

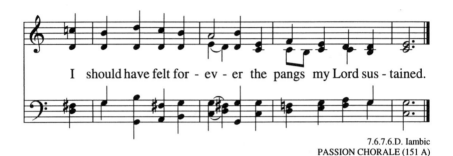

I should have felt for - ev - er the pangs my Lord sus - tained.

7.6.7.6.D. Iambic
PASSION CHORALE (151 A)

79 Suddenly, one of those with Jesus put his hand on his sword, drew it, and struck the slave of the high priest, cutting off his ear. Then Jesus said to him, "Put your sword back into its place; for all who take the sword will perish by the sword. Do you think that I cannot appeal to my Father, and he will at once send me more than twelve legions of angels? But how then would the scriptures be fulfilled, which say it must happen in this way?"

At that hour Jesus said to the crowds, "Have you come out with swords and clubs to arrest me as though I were a bandit? Day after day I sat in the temple teaching, and you did not arrest me. But all this has taken place, so that the scriptures of the prophets may be fulfilled."

Then all the disciples deserted him and fled. A certain young man was following him, wearing nothing but a linen cloth. They caught hold of him, but he left the linen cloth and ran off naked.

Lord, may we not fall a-way fail-ing in our lives to pray.

Keep us close to your blessed side, there may we in love a-bide;

ev-er with the ran-somed sing grate-ful prais-es to our King.

7.7.7.7.7.7.
RATISBON

Jesus' Trial before Jewish Authorities
John 18:12-14, 18-24; 26:59-68

80 So the soldiers, their officer, and the Jewish police arrested Jesus and bound him. First they took him to Annas, who was the father-in-law of Caiaphas, the high priest that year. Caiaphas was the one who had advised the Jews that it was better to have one person die for the people.

Then the high priest questioned Jesus about his disciples and about his teaching. Jesus answered, "I have spoken openly to the world; I have always taught in synagogues and in the temple, where all the Jews come together. I have said nothing in secret. Why do you ask me? Ask those who heard what I said to them; they know what I said."

When he had said this, one of the police standing nearby struck Jesus on the face, saying, "Is that how you answer the high priest?"

Jesus answered, "If I have spoken wrongly, testify to the wrong. But if I have spoken rightly, why do you strike me?" Then Annas sent him bound to Caiaphas the high priest.

1 O dear-est Je - sus, what law have you bro - ken
2 How strange is this great par - a - dox to pon - der:

that such sharp sen - tence should on you be
the shep - herd dies for sheep who love to

spo - ken? Of what great crime have you to make con-
wan - der; the mas - ter pays the debt his ser - vants

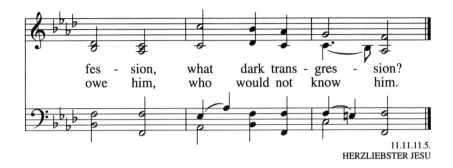

fes - sion, what dark trans - gres - sion?
owe him, who would not know him.

11.11.11.5.
HERZLIEBSTER JESU

81 Now the slaves and the police had made a charcoal fire because it was cold, and they were standing around it and warming themselves. Peter also was standing with them and warming himself.

Now the chief priests and the whole council were looking for false testimony against Jesus so that they might put him to death, but they found none, though many false witnesses came forward.

At last two came forward and said, "This fellow said, 'I am able to destroy the temple of God and to build it in three days.' "

The high priest stood up and said, "Have you no answer? What is it that they testify against you?" But Jesus was silent. Then the high priest said to him, "I put you under oath before the living God, tell us if you are the Messiah, the Son of God."

Jesus said to him, "You have said so. But I tell you, from now on you will see the Son of Man seated at the right hand of Power and coming on the clouds of heaven."

82 Then the high priest tore his clothes and said, "He has blasphemed! Why do we still need witness-

es? You have now heard his blasphemy. What is your verdict?"

They answered, "He deserves death."

Then they spat in his face and struck him; and some slapped him, saying, "Prophesy to us, you Messiah! Who is it that struck you?"

Lord, your deep hu - mil - i - a - tion has a - toned for all my pride; I need fear no con - dem - na - tion since for sin - ners you have died. You be - came a curse, dear Sav - ior, to re - store me to God's fa - vor; thou - sand, thou - sand

thanks are due dear-est Je-sus, un-to you.

8.7.8.7.8.8.7.7. Trochaic
ZURICH (168 A)

Peter's Denial of Jesus
Matthew 26:69-75

Now Peter was sitting outside in the court-yard. A servant-girl came to him and said, "You also were with Jesus the Galilean." But he denied it before all of them, saying, "I do not know what you are talking about."

When he went out to the porch, another ser-vant-girl saw him, and she said to the bystanders, "This man was with Jesus of Nazareth."

83 Again he denied it with an oath, "I do not know the man."

After a little while the bystanders came up and said to Peter, "Certainly you are also one of them, for your accent betrays you."

Then he began to curse, and he swore an oath, "I do not know the man!" At that moment the cock crowed.

Then Peter remembered what Jesus had said: "Before the cock crows, you will deny me three times." And he went out and wept bitterly.

1 In the hour of tri - al, Je - sus, plead for me;
2 When my last hour com - eth, fraught with strife and pain,

lest by base de - ni - al I de-part from thee;
when my dust re - turn - eth to the dust a - gain,

when thou seest me wa - ver, with a look re - call,
on thy truth re - ly - ing through that mor - tal strife,

nor for fear or fa - vor suf - fer me to fall.
Je - sus, take me, dy - ing, to e - ter - nal life.

6.5.6.5.D.
PENITENCE (141 E)

Friday

Jesus before the Council
Luke 22:66-71

84 When day came, the assembly of the elders of the people, both chief priests and scribes, gathered together, and they brought Jesus to their council. They said, "If you are the Messiah, tell us."

He replied, "If I tell you, you will not believe; and if I question you, you will not answer. But from now on the Son of Man will be seated at the right hand of the power of God."

All of them asked, "Are you, then, the Son of God?"

He said to them, "You say that I am."

Then they said, "What further testimony do we need? We have heard it ourselves from his own lips!"

Judas Takes His Own Life
Matthew 27:3-10

When Judas, his betrayer, saw that Jesus was condemned, he repented and brought back the thirty pieces of silver to the chief priests and the elders. He said, "I have sinned by betraying innocent blood."

But they said, "What is that to us? See to it yourself."

85 Throwing down the pieces of silver in the temple, he departed; and he went and hanged himself.

But the chief priests, taking the pieces of silver, said, "It is not lawful to put them into the treasury, since they are blood money." After conferring together, they used them to buy the potter's field as a place to bury foreigners. For this reason that field has been called the Field of Blood to this day. Then was fulfilled what had been spoken through the prophet Jeremiah, "And they took the thirty pieces of silver, the price of the one on whom a price had been set, on whom some of the people of Israel had set a price, and they gave them for the potter's field, as the Lord commanded me."

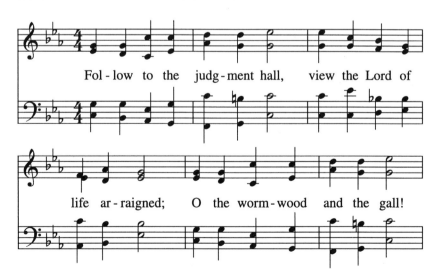

Fol - low to the judg-ment hall, view the Lord of life ar - raigned; O the worm-wood and the gall!

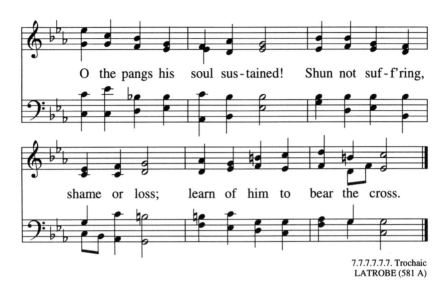

O the pangs his soul sus-tained! Shun not suf-f'ring,

shame or loss; learn of him to bear the cross.

7.7.7.7.7.7. Trochaic
LATROBE (581 A)

The Trial before Pilate
Matthew 27:12-24; Luke 23:2;
John 18:28-38

Then they took Jesus from Caiaphas to Pilate's headquarters. It was early in the morning. They themselves did not enter the headquarters, so as to avoid ritual defilement and to be able to eat the Passover.

86 So Pilate went out to them and said, "What accusation do you bring against this man?"

They answered, "If this man were not a criminal, we would not have handed him over to you."

Pilate said to them, "Take him yourselves and judge him according to your law."

The Jews replied, "We are not permitted to put anyone to death." (This was to fulfill what Jesus had said when he indicated the kind of death he was to die.)

The cross, the cross, O, that's my gain, be -
cause on that the Lamb was slain; 'twas there my Lord was
cru - ci - fied, 'twas there my Sav - ior for me died.

L.M.
RHAW (22 A)

They began to accuse him, saying, "We found this man perverting our nation, forbidding us to pay taxes to the emperor, and saying that he himself is the Messiah, a king."

Then Pilate entered the headquarters again, summoned Jesus, and asked him, "Are you the King of the Jews?"

Jesus answered, "Do you ask this on your own, or did others tell you about me?"

87 Pilate replied, "I am not a Jew, am I? Your own nation and the chief priests have handed you over to me. What have you done?" Jesus answered,

"My kingdom is not from this world. If my kingdom were from this world, my followers would be fighting to keep me from being handed over to the Jews. But as it is, my kingdom is not from here."

Pilate asked him, "So you are a king?"

Hail, O once de - spis-ed Je-sus! Hail, O Gal-i - le-an King!

You have suf-fered to re - lease us, hope, sal - va - tion,

joy to bring. Hail, O ag - o - niz - ing Sav - ior,

bear - er of our sin and shame; by your mer - its

we find fa - vor; life is giv - en through your name.

8.7.8.7.D. Trochaic
CASSEL (167 A)

Jesus answered, "You say that I am a king. For this I was born, and for this I came into the world, to testify to the truth. Everyone who belongs to the truth listens to my voice."

Pilate asked him, "What is truth?"

After he had said this, he went out to the Jews again and told them, "I find no case against him."

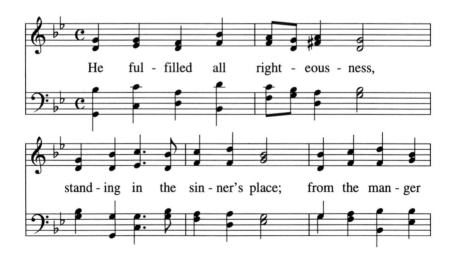

He ful - filled all right - eous - ness,

stand - ing in the sin - ner's place; from the man - ger

to the cross, all he did, he did for us.

7.7.7.7.
NUN KOMM, DER HEIDEN HEILAND (11 D)

88 When he was accused by the chief priests and elders, he did not answer. Then Pilate said to him, "Do you not hear how many accusations they make against you?"

But he gave him no answer, not even to a single charge, so that the governor was greatly amazed.

Jesus before Herod
Luke 23:4-16

Then Pilate said to the chief priests and the crowds, "I find no basis for an accusation against this man."

But they were insistent and said, "He stirs up the people by teaching throughout all Judea, from Galilee where he began even to this place."

89 When Pilate heard this, he asked whether the man was a Galilean. And when he learned that he was under Herod's jurisdiction, he sent him off to Herod, who was himself in Jerusalem at that time. When Herod saw Jesus, he was very glad, for he had been wanting to see him for a long time, because he had heard about him and was hoping to see him per-

form some sign. He questioned him at some length, but Jesus gave him no answer. The chief priests and the scribes stood by, vehemently accusing him. Even Herod with his soldiers treated him with contempt and mocked him; then he put an elegant robe on him, and sent him back to Pilate.

That same day Herod and Pilate became friends with each other; before this they had been enemies.

Pilate then called together the chief priests, the leaders, and the people, and said to them, "You brought me this man as one who was perverting the people; and here I have examined him in your presence and have not found this man guilty of any of your charges against him. Neither has Herod, for he sent him back to us. Indeed, he has done nothing to deserve death. I will therefore have him flogged and release him."

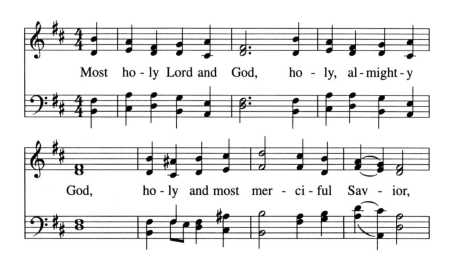

Most ho-ly Lord and God, ho - ly, al-might-y God, ho-ly and most mer - ci-ful Sav - ior,

our e - ter - nal God!   Lamb of God un - spot - ted,

to our prayers, O   lend an ear.   Have mer - cy, O   Lord.

6.6.9.5.6.7.5.
EISLEBEN (519 A)

Barabbas or Jesus
Matthew 27:15-25

90 Now at the festival the governor was accustomed to release a prisoner for the crowd, anyone whom they wanted. At that time they had a notorious prisoner, called Jesus Barabbas. So after they had gathered, Pilate said to them, "Whom do you want me to release for you, Jesus Barabbas or Jesus who is called the Messiah?"

For he realized that it was out of jealousy that they had handed him over. While he was sitting on the judgment seat, his wife sent word to him, "Have nothing to do with that innocent man, for today I have suffered a great deal because of a dream about him." Now the chief priests and the elders persuaded the crowds to ask for Barabbas and to have Jesus killed. The governor again said to them, "Which of the two do you want me to release for you?"

And they said, "Barabbas."

Pilate said to them, "Then what should I do with Jesus who is called the Messiah?"

All of them said, "Let him be crucified!"

Then he asked, "Why, what evil has he done?"

But they shouted all the more, "Let him be crucified!"

Christ, the life of all the liv-ing, Christ, the death of death, our foe, Christ, for us your-self once giv-ing to the dark-est depths of woe: through your suf-f'ring, death, and mer-it, life e-ter-nal we in-her-it; thou-sand, thou-sand

thanks are due, dear-est Je-sus, un-to you.

8.7.8.7.8.8.7.7. Trochaic
ZURICH (168 A)

91 So when Pilate saw that he could do nothing, but rather that a riot was beginning, he took some water and washed his hands before the crowd, saying, "I am innocent of this man's blood; see to it yourselves."

Then the people as a whole answered, "His blood be on us and on our children!"

The Crucifixion
Matthew 27:26-44; Mark 15:20-41;
Luke 23:27-48; John 19:4-37

So he released Barabbas for them; and after flogging Jesus, he handed him over to be crucified.

Then the soldiers of the governor took Jesus into the governor's headquarters, and they gathered the whole cohort around him. They stripped him and put a scarlet robe on him, and after twisting some thorns into a crown, they put it on his head. They put a reed in his right hand and knelt before him and mocked him, saying, "Hail, King of the Jews!" They spat on him, and took the reed and struck him on the head.

7.6.7.6.D. Iambic
PASSION CHORALE (151 A)

Pilate went out again and said to them, "Look, I am bringing him out to you to let you know that I find no case against him." So Jesus came out, wearing the crown of thorns and the purple robe. Pilate said to them, "Here is the man!"

Sing with awe in strains mel - o - dious, sing with awe: "Here is the Man!" Yes, re - peat in tones har - mon - ious, "Ah! Be - hold, here is the Man!"

8.7.8.7. Trochaic
ZURICH (168 A), part 1

When the chief priests and the police saw him, they shouted, "Crucify him! Crucify him!"

Pilate said to them, "Take him yourselves and crucify him; I find no case against him."

The Jews answered him, "We have a law, and according to that law he ought to die because he has claimed to be the Son of God."

93 Now when Pilate heard this, he was more afraid than ever. He entered his headquarters again and asked Jesus, "Where are you from?"

But Jesus gave him no answer. Pilate therefore said to him, "Do you refuse to speak to me? Do you not know that I have power to release you, and power to crucify you?"

Jesus answered him, "You would have no power over me unless it had been given you from above; therefore the one who handed me over to you is guilty of a greater sin."

From then on Pilate tried to release him, but the Jews cried out, "If you release this man, you are no friend of the emperor. Everyone who claims to be a king sets himself against the emperor."

When Pilate heard these words, he brought Jesus outside and sat on the judge's bench at a place called The Stone Pavement, or in Hebrew Gabbatha. Now it was the day of Preparation for the Passover; and it was about noon.

He said to the Jews, "Here is your King!"

They cried out, "Away with him! Away with him! Crucify him!"

Pilate asked them, "Shall I crucify your King?"

The chief priests answered, "We have no king but the emperor."

Then he handed him over to them to be crucified.

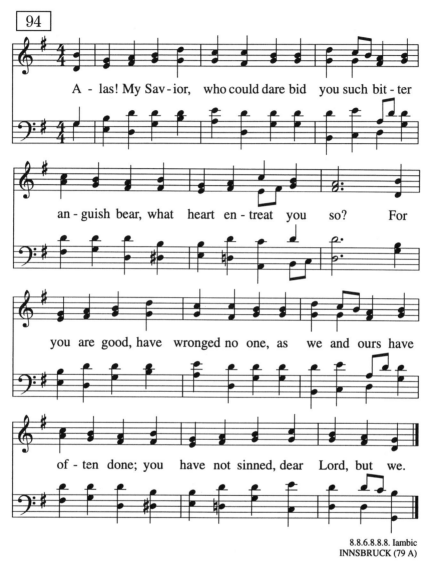

A - las! My Sav - ior, who could dare bid you such bit - ter

an - guish bear, what heart en - treat you so? For

you are good, have wronged no one, as we and ours have

of - ten done; you have not sinned, dear Lord, but we.

8.8.6.8.8.8. Iambic
INNSBRUCK (79 A)

After mocking him, they stripped him of the purple cloak and put his own clothes on him. Then they led him out to crucify him.

They compelled a passer-by, who was coming in from the country, to carry his cross; it was Simon of Cyrene, the father of Alexander and Rufus.

Must Je - sus bear the cross a - lone, and all the world go free? No, there's a cross for ev - 'ry one, and there's a cross for me.

C.M.
MAITLAND

95 A great number of the people followed him, and among them were women who were stricken with grief for him. But Jesus turned to them and said, "Daughters of Jerusalem, do not weep for me, but weep for yourselves and for your children. For the days are surely coming when they will say, 'Blessed are the barren, and the wombs that never bore, and the breasts that never nursed.' Then they will begin to say to the mountains, 'Fall on us'; and to the hills, 'Cover us.' For if they do this when the wood is green, what will happen when it is dry?"

Two others also, who were criminals, were led away to be put to death with him. When they came to the place that is called The Skull, they crucified Jesus there with the criminals, one on his right and one on his left.

Then Jesus said, "Father, forgive them; for they do not know what they are doing."

Hark, his dy - ing word: "For - give:
Fa - ther, let the sin - ner live; sin - ner, wipe your
tears a - way, I your ran - som free - ly pay."

7.7.7.7.
NUN KOMM, DER HEIDEN HEILAND (11 D)

When the soldiers had crucified Jesus, they took his clothes and divided them into four parts, one for each soldier. They also took his tunic; now the tunic was seamless, woven in one piece from the top. So they said to one another, "Let us not tear it, but cast lots for it to see who will get it." This was to fulfill what the scripture says,

"They divided my clothes among themselves, and for my clothing they cast lots."

96

Be - neath the cross of Je - sus I fain would take my stand; the shad-ow of a might-y rock with - in a wea-ry land; O bless - ed shel - ter from the storm, the sin - ner's sure re - treat; O tryst - ing place, where heav'n - ly love and heav'n - ly jus - tice meet.

7.6.8.6.8.6.8.6.
ST. CHRISTOPHER

It was nine o'clock in the morning when they crucified him.

Pilate also had an inscription written and put on the cross. It read, "Jesus of Nazareth, the King of the Jews." Many of the Jews read this inscription, because the place where Jesus was crucified was near the city; and it was written in Hebrew, in Latin, and in Greek. Then the chief priests of the Jews said to Pilate, "Do not write, 'The King of the Jews,' but, 'This man said, I am King of the Jews.'"

Pilate answered, "What I have written I have written."

The truth, that Da-vid learned to sing, its deep ful-fill-ment here at-tains: "Tell all the earth, the Lord is King!" Lo, from the cross, a king he reigns.

L.M.
DUKE STREET (22 Q)

97 Those who passed by derided him, shaking their heads and saying, "You who would destroy the temple and build it in three days, save yourself! If you are the Son of God, come down from the cross." And the people stood by, watching.

1 When to the cross I turn my eyes, and
2 Re - mem - ber thee, and all thy pains, and
3 And when these fail - ing limbs grow numb, and

rest on Cal - va - ry, O Lamb of God, my
all thy love to me? Yea, while a breath, a
mind and mem - 'ry flee, when thou shalt in thy

sac - ri - fice, I must re - mem - ber thee.
pulse re - mains will I re - mem - ber thee.
king - dom come, Je - sus, re - mem - ber me.

C.M.
HAB DANK, O JESU

In the same way the chief priests also, along with the scribes and elders, were mocking him, saying, "He saved others; he cannot save himself. He is the King of Israel; let him come down from the cross now, and we will believe in him. He trusts in God; let God deliver him now, if he wants to; for he said, 'I am God's Son.' "

The bandits who were crucified with him also taunted him in the same way.

98

1 A - round that cross the crowd I see, mock -
2 'Twas I that shed the sa - cred blood, I

ing the suf-f'rer's groan; yet still my voice it
nailed him to the tree, I cru - ci - fied the

seems to be, as if I mocked a - lone.
Christ of God, I joined the mock - er - y.

C.M.
ESSLINGEN (14 A)

One of the criminals who were hanged there kept deriding him and saying, "Are you not the Messiah? Save yourself and us!"

But the other rebuked him, saying, "Do you not fear God, since you are under the same sen-tence of condemnation? And we indeed have been condemned justly, for we are getting what we deserve for our deeds, but this man has done nothing wrong."

Then he said, "Jesus, remember me when you come into your kingdom."

He replied, "Truly I tell you, today you will be with me in Paradise."

Meanwhile, standing near the cross of Jesus were his mother, and his mother's sister, Mary the wife of Clopas, and Mary Magdalene.

99

Near the cross was Mar-y weep-ing, there her mourn-ful sta-tion keep-ing, gaz-ing on her dy-ing son.

There with speech-less grief op-press-ed, an-guish-strick-en,

and dis - tress - ed, through her soul the sword had gone.

8.8.7.8.8.7. Trochaic
STABAT MATER (95 C)

When Jesus saw his mother and the disciple whom he loved standing beside her, he said to his mother, "Woman, here is your son." Then he said to the disciple, "Here is your mother." And from that hour the disciple took her into his own home.

Grant me to lean un - sha - ken up - on your faith - ful - ness,

un - til I hence am ta - ken, to see you face to face.

7.6.7.6. Iambic
PASSION CHORALE (151 A), part 2

When it was noon, darkness came over the whole land until three in the afternoon. At three o'clock Jesus cried out with a loud voice, "Eloi, Eloi, lema sabachthani?" which means, "My God, my God, why have you forsaken me?"

100

Up - on the cross of Je - sus, my eye by faith can

see the ver - y dy - ing form of one who

suf - fered there for me. And from my con - trite

heart, with tears, two won - ders I con - fess: the

won - der of his glo - rious love and my un - wor - thi - ness.

7.6.8.6.8.6.8.6.
ST. CHRISTOPHER

When some of the bystanders heard it, they said,
"Listen, he is calling for Elijah."

After this, when Jesus knew that all was now finished, he said (in order to fulfill the scripture), "I am thirsty."

A jar full of sour wine was standing there. So they put a sponge full of the wine on a branch of hyssop and held it to his mouth.

When Jesus had received the wine, he said, "It is finished."

1 "It is fin - ished!" Shall we raise
2 Lamb of God! Your death has giv'n

songs of sor - row, or of praise? Mourn to see the
par - don, peace, and hope of heav'n. "It is fin - ished!"

Sav - ior die, or pro - claim his vic - to - ry?
Let us raise songs of thank - ful - ness and praise.

7.7.7.7.
NUN KOMM, DER HEIDEN HEILAND (11 D)

(Standing)

101 Then Jesus, crying with a loud voice, said, "Father, into your hands I commend my spirit." Having said this, he breathed his last.

(Sitting or kneeling)

Silent Prayer

(During the silent prayer, the choir may sing:)

Most ho - ly Lord and God, ho - ly, al - might - y God, ho - ly and most mer - ci - ful Sav - ior, our e - ter - nal God! Grant that we may nev - er

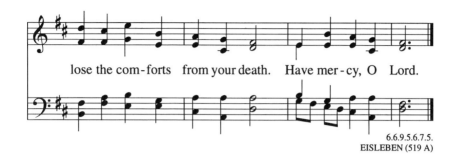

lose the com-forts   from your death.   Have mer-cy, O   Lord.

6.6.9.5.6.7.5.
EISLEBEN (519 A)

By your cross and suffering,
By your sacred wounds and precious blood,
By your dying words,
By your atoning death,
Bless and comfort us, gracious Lord
and God.

(Sitting)

102 At that moment the curtain of the temple was torn in two, from top to bottom. The earth shook, and the rocks were split. The tombs also were opened, and many bodies of the saints who had fallen asleep were raised. After his resurrection they came out of the tombs and entered the holy city and appeared to many.

Now when the centurion and those with him, who were keeping watch over Jesus, saw the earthquake and what took place, they were terrified and said, "Truly this man was God's Son!"

God and man in - deed, com-fort in all need,
you be-came a Man of sor-rows to gain life e - ter-nal for us
by your pre - cious blood, Je - sus, man and God.

5.5.8.8.5.5. Trochaic
SEELENBRÄUTIGAM (68 A)

And when all the crowds who had gathered there for this spectacle saw what had taken place, they returned home, beating their breasts.

There were also women looking on from a distance; among them were Mary Magdalene, and Mary the mother of James the younger and of Joses, and Salome. These used to follow him and provided for him when he was in Galilee; and there were many other women who had come up with him to Jerusalem.

103 Since it was the day of Preparation, the Jews did not want the bodies left on the cross during the Sabbath, especially because that Sabbath was a day

of great solemnity. So they asked Pilate to have the legs of the crucified men broken and the bodies removed. Then the soldiers came and broke the legs of the first and of the other who had been crucified with him. But when they came to Jesus and saw that he was already dead, they did not break his legs. Instead, one of the soldiers pierced his side with a spear, and at once blood and water came out.

Rock of A-ges, cleft for me! Let me hide my-self in thee;

let the wa-ter and the blood, from thy ri-ven side which flowed,

be of sin the dou-ble cure, cleanse me from its guilt and pow'r.

7.7.7.7.7.7. Trochaic
GRACEHAM (581 K)

(He who saw this has testified so that you also may believe. His testimony is true, and he knows that he tells the truth.) These things occurred so that the scripture might be fulfilled, "None of his bones shall be broken." And again another passage of scripture says, "They will look on the one whom they have pierced."

104

A Voice: On - ly one prayer to - day, one
Choir: Be - cause of Je - sus' cross, and
Congregation: No oth - er name than his my

ear - nest tear - ful plea, a lit - a - ny from
that un - fath - omed sea, the crim - son tide which
hope, my help may be; O by that one all -

out the heart, "Have mer - cy, Lord, on me!"
heals the world, "Have mer - cy, Lord, on me!"
sav - ing name, "Have mer - cy, Lord, on me!"

S.M.
AYLESBURY (582 A)

The Burial
Mark 15:42-45; Luke 23:55-56;
John 19:39-42

When evening had come, and since it was the day of Preparation, that is, the day before the Sabbath, Joseph of Arimathea, a respected member of the council, who was also himself waiting expectantly for the kingdom of God, went boldly to Pilate and asked for the body of Jesus. Then Pilate wondered if he were already dead; and summoning the centurion, he asked him whether he had been dead for some time. When he learned from the centurion that he was dead, he granted the body to Joseph.

105 Nicodemus, who had at first come to Jesus by night, also came, bringing a mixture of myrrh and aloes, weighing about a hundred pounds. They took the body of Jesus and wrapped it with the spices in linen cloths, according to the burial custom of the Jews. Now there was a garden in the place where he was crucified, and in the garden there was a new tomb in which no one had ever been laid. And so, because it was the Jewish day of Preparation, and the tomb was nearby, they laid Jesus there.

1 Lord of life! Now sweet-ly slum-ber, with the dead a -
2 O, what love is here dis-play-ed! See the Fa-ther's

while a guest; af-ter tor-ments with-out num-ber, glo-rious is your
on - ly son   to the si-lent tomb con-vey-ed;   ah, my soul, what

hard-earned rest;   Lo! The dread-ful   con-flict's end-ed;
have   you done!   Yet, while   I,   my   sins   be-wail-ing,

by   your suf-f'rings   you have won;   o - ver   all   your
own that they   his   blood have spilt,   may   that blood, for

pow'r's ex - tend - ed;   take   my heart, O   claim your own.
me   pre - vail - ing,   wash a - way   my   sins   and guilt.

8.7.8.7.D. Trochaic
CASSEL (167 A)

106 The women who had come with him from
Galilee followed, and they saw the tomb and how
his body was laid. Then they returned, and prepared
spices and ointments.

On the Sabbath they rested according to the
commandment.

The Watch at the Tomb
Matthew 27:62-66

The next day, that is, after the day of Preparation, the chief priests and the Pharisees gathered before Pilate and said, "Sir, we remember what that impostor said while he was still alive, 'After three days I will rise again.' Therefore command the tomb to be made secure until the third day; otherwise his disciples may go and steal him away, and tell the people, 'He has been raised from the dead,' and the last deception would be worse than the first."

Pilate said to them, "You have a guard of soldiers; go, make it as secure as you can."

So they went with the guard and made the tomb secure by sealing the stone.

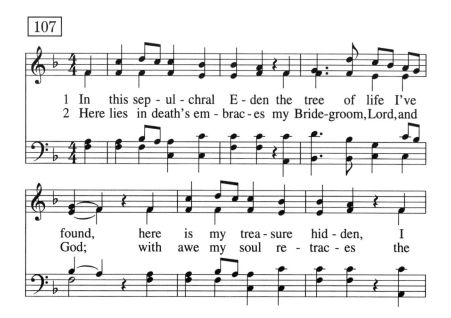

1 In this sep - ul - chral E - den the tree of life I've
2 Here lies in death's em - brac - es my Bride-groom, Lord, and

found, here is my trea - sure hid - den, I
God; with awe my soul re - trac - es the

tread on hal - lowed ground.   You   sick,   you faint and
dark   and dol - 'rous   road   that   leads   to   this   last

wea - ry,   though   all   your ail - ments   var - y,   come
sta - tion;   here   in   sweet med - i - ta - tion   I'll

hith - er, and make   sure   of   a most per - fect   cure.
dwell by day   and   night,   till   faith is changed to   sight.

7.6.7.6.7.7.6.6. Iambic
EDEN (597 B)

Or

1 The grave to-day is hold-ing our Lord, our life, our love;
2 Your Sab-bath-rest, dear Sav-ior, we cel-e-brate with joy;

with-in its depths en-fold-ing the heights of heav'n a-bove.
to praise its sol-emn splen-dor our high-est gifts em-ploy.

In death, most gra-cious Sav-ior, you proved our dear-est Friend,
Lead us to rise vic-to-rious, as you burst bonds of hell,

the on-ly path which leads us to life which knows no end.
to join in hymns most glo-rious your sav-ing pow'r to tell.

© C. Daniel Crews

7.6.7.6.D. Iambic
PASSION CHORALE (151 A)

The Resurrection

109

1 Christ is a - live! Let Chris - tians sing. The cross stands
2 Christ is a - live! No long - er bound to dis - tant
3 Christ is a - live, and comes to bring good news to

emp - ty to the sky. Let streets and homes with
years in Pal - es - tine, but sav - ing, heal - ing,
this and ev - 'ry age, till earth and sky and

prais - es ring. Love, drowned in death, shall nev - er die.
here and now, and touch - ing ev - 'ry place and time.
o - cean ring with joy, with jus - tice, love, and praise.

L.M.
TRURO

Appearances at the Tomb
Mark 16:1-8; Matthew 28:2-4, 9-10;
John 20:2-18; Luke 24:11

When the Sabbath was over, Mary Magdalene, and Mary the mother of James, and Salome bought spices, so that they might go and anoint him. And very early on the first day of the week, when the sun had risen, they went to the tomb.

110 And suddenly there was a great earthquake; for an angel of the Lord, descending from heaven, came and rolled back the stone and sat on it. His appearance was like lightning, and his clothing white as snow. For fear of him the guards shook and became like dead men.

The women had been saying to one another, "Who will roll away the stone for us from the entrance to the tomb?" When they looked up, they saw that the stone, which was very large, had already been rolled back.

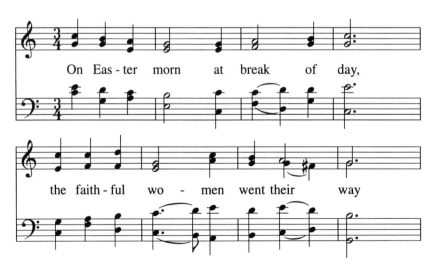

On Eas - ter morn at break of day,

the faith - ful wo - men went their way

to seek the tomb where Je - sus lay.

Al - le - lu - ia, ____ al - le - lu - ia, ____ al - le - lu - ia.

8.8.8. with Alleluias
GELOBT SEI GOTT

As they entered the tomb, they saw a young man, dressed in a white robe, sitting on the right side; and they were alarmed.

But he said to them, "Do not be alarmed; you are looking for Jesus of Nazareth, who was crucified. He has been raised; he is not here. Look, there is the place they laid him." So they went out and fled from the tomb, for terror and amazement had seized them.

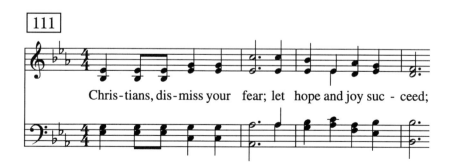

111

Chris - tians, dis - miss your fear; let hope and joy suc - ceed;

the joy-ful news with glad-ness hear:"The Lord is ris'n in-deed!"

The prom-ise is ful-filled in Christ our on-ly Head;

now jus-tice, mer-cy, rec-on-ciled,he lives who once was dead.

S.M.D.
DIADEMATA (595 C)

Mary Magdalene ran to Simon Peter and the other disciple, the one whom Jesus loved, and said to them, "They have taken the Lord out of the tomb, and we do not know where they have laid him." But these words seemed to them an idle tale, and they did not believe them.

Then Peter and the other disciple set out and went toward the tomb. The two were running together, but the other disciple outran Peter and reached the tomb first. He bent down to look in and saw the linen wrappings lying there, but he did not go in. Then Simon Peter came, following him, and

went into the tomb. He saw the linen wrappings
lying there, and the cloth that had been on Jesus'
head, not lying with the linen wrappings but rolled
up in a place by itself. Then the other disciple, who
reached the tomb first, also went in, and he saw
and believed; for as yet they did not understand the
scripture, that he must rise from the dead. Then the
disciples returned to their homes.

112

O mourn-ing souls, dry up your tears; dis-miss your
gloom-y doubts and fears; with cheer-ful hope your
hearts re - vive, for Christ, the Lord, is now a - live.

L.M.
DUKE STREET (22 Q)

But Mary stood weeping outside the tomb.
As she wept, she bent over to look into the tomb;
and she saw two angels in white, sitting where the
body of Jesus had been lying, one at the head and

the other at the feet.

They said to her, "Woman, why are you weeping?"

She said to them, "They have taken away my Lord, and I do not know where they have laid him."

When she had said this, she turned around and saw Jesus standing there, but she did not know that it was Jesus. Jesus said to her, "Woman, why are you weeping? Whom are you looking for?"

Supposing him to be the gardener, she said to him, "Sir, if you have carried him away, tell me where you have laid him, and I will take him away."

Jesus said to her, "Mary!"

She turned and said to him in Hebrew, "Rabbouni!" (which means Teacher).

113 Jesus said to her, "Do not hold on to me, because I have not yet ascended to the Father. But go to my brothers and say to them, 'I am ascending to my Father and your Father, to my God and your God.' "

Mary Magdalene went and announced to the disciples, "I have seen the Lord"; and she told them that he had said these things to her.

Je - sus Christ is ris'n to - day, al - le - lu - ia!

Our tri-um-phant ho-ly day, al - le - lu - ia!

Who did once, up - on the cross, al - le - lu - ia!

Suf - fer to re - deem our loss. Al - le - lu - ia!

7.7.7.7. with Alleluias
WORGAN (11 W)

Report of the Guards
Matthew 28:11-15

Jesus met the women and said, "Greetings!" And they came to him, took hold of his feet, and worshiped him.

Then Jesus said to them, "Do not be afraid; go and tell my brothers to go to Galilee; there they will see me."

While they were going, some of the guard went into the city and told the chief priests everything that had happened.

114 After the priests had assembled with the elders, they devised a plan to give a large sum of money to the soldiers, telling them, "You must say, 'His disciples came by night and stole him away while we were asleep.' If this comes to the governor's ears, we will satisfy him and keep you out of trouble."

So they took the money and did as they were directed.

Ear-ly has-ten to the tomb, where they laid his breath-less clay;
all is sol-i-tude and gloom; who has tak-en him a-way?
Christ is ris'n – he meets our eyes! Sav-ior, teach us so to rise.

7.7.7.7.7.7. Trochaic
LATROBE (581 A)

Appearance on the Way to Emmaus
Luke 24:13-35

Now on that same day two of them were going to a village called Emmaus, about seven miles from Jerusalem, and talking with each other about all these things that had happened. While they were talking and discussing, Jesus himself came near and went with them, but their eyes were kept from recognizing him.

And he said to them, "What are you discussing with each other while you walk along?"

They stood still, looking sad. Then one of them, whose name was Cleopas, answered him, "Are you the only stranger in Jerusalem who does not know the things that have taken place there in these days?"

115 He asked them, "What things?"

They replied, "The things about Jesus of Nazareth, who was a prophet mighty in deed and word before God and all the people, and how our chief priests and leaders handed him over to be condemned to death and crucified him. But we had hoped that he was the one to redeem Israel. Yes, and besides all this, it is now the third day since these things took place. Moreover, some women of our group astounded us. They were at the tomb early this morning, and when they did not find his body there, they came back and told us that they had indeed seen a vision of angels who said that he was alive. Some of those who were with us went to the tomb and found it just as the women had said;

but they did not see him."

Then he said to them, "Oh, how foolish you are, and how slow of heart to believe all that the prophets have declared! Was it not necessary that the Messiah should suffer these things and then enter into his glory?" Then beginning with Moses and all the prophets, he interpreted to them the things about himself in all the scriptures.

As they came near the village to which they were going, he walked ahead as if he were going on. But they urged him strongly, saying, "Stay with us, because it is almost evening and the day is now nearly over." So he went in to stay with them.

116

No far-ther go to - night, but stay, dear Sav-ior, till the break of day; "A - bide, my Lord, with me." And in the morn-ing when I wake, me un - der thy pro-

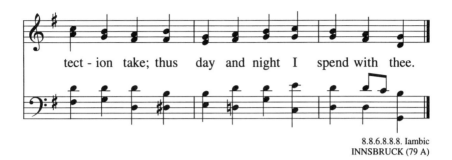

tect - ion take; thus day and night I spend with thee.

8.8.6.8.8.8. Iambic
INNSBRUCK (79 A)

When he was at the table with them, he took bread, blessed and broke it, and gave it to them. Then their eyes were opened, and they recognized him; and he vanished from their sight.

They said to each other, "Were not our hearts burning within us while he was talking to us on the road, while he was opening the scriptures to us?"

That same hour they got up and returned to Jerusalem; and they found the eleven and their companions gathered together. They were saying, "The Lord has risen indeed, and he has appeared to Simon!"

Then they told what had happened on the road, and how Jesus had been made known to them in the breaking of the bread.

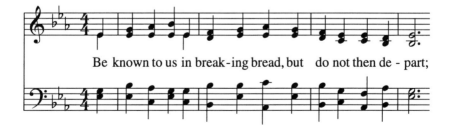

Be known to us in break-ing bread, but do not then de - part;

Sav - ior, a-bide with us, and spread your ta-ble in our heart.

C.M.
DUNDEE (14 P)

Jesus Appears to His Disciples
John 20:19-29; Luke 24:37-48

117 When it was evening on that day, the first day of the week, and the doors of the house where the disciples had met were locked for fear of the Jews, Jesus came and stood among them and said, "Peace be with you."

All hail, our church's El - der dear, O

Je - sus, glo - rious head! To your dis - ci - ples

now ap-pear as ris - en from the dead. Let our re-joic-ing

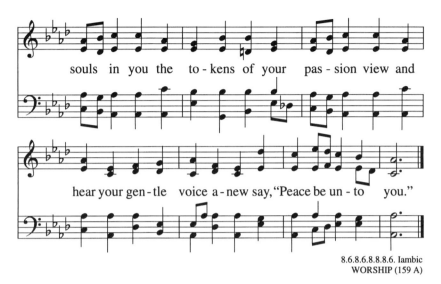

souls in you the to-kens of your pas-sion view and

hear your gen-tle voice a-new say, "Peace be un-to you."

8.6.8.6.8.8.8.6. Iambic
WORSHIP (159 A)

They were startled and terrified, and thought that they were seeing a ghost. He said to them, "Why are you frightened, and why do doubts arise in your hearts? Look at my hands and my feet; see that it is I myself. Touch me and see; for a ghost does not have flesh and bones as you see that I have." And when he had said this, he showed them his hands and his feet.

While in their joy they were disbelieving and still wondering, he said to them, "Have you anything here to eat?" They gave him a piece of broiled fish, and he took it and ate in their presence.

118 Then he said to them, "These are my words that I spoke to you while I was still with you — that everything written about me in the law of Moses, the prophets, and the psalms must be fulfilled."

Then he opened their minds to understand the scriptures, and he said to them, "Thus it is written, that the Messiah is to suffer and to rise from the dead on the third day, and that repentance and forgiveness of sins is to be proclaimed in his name to all nations, beginning from Jerusalem. You are witnesses of these things."

1 Wit - ness here to all a - round you of your
2 Ev - i - dence by word and ac - tion that your

Sav - ior's dy - ing love; tell them how he sought and
faith is not in vain, that your high - est sat - is -

found you, gave you grace from heav'n a - bove.
fac - tion cen - ters in the Lamb once slain.

8.7.8.7. Trochaic
BATTY (16 A)

Jesus said to them again, "Peace be with you. As the Father has sent me, so I send you."

When he had said this, he breathed on them and said to them, "Receive the Holy Spirit. If you forgive the sins of any, they are forgiven them; if you retain the sins of any, they are retained."

119

Peace be to this con - gre - ga - tion, peace to ev - 'ry

soul there - in; peace, which flows from Christ's sal - va - tion,

peace, the seal of can - celled sin, peace that speaks its

heav'n - ly Giv - er, peace, to earth - ly minds un - known,

peace di - vine that lasts for - ev - er here e - rect its glo - rious throne.

8.7.8.7.D. Trochaic
CASSEL (167 A)

But Thomas (who was called the Twin), one of the twelve, was not with them when Jesus came.

But he said to them, "Unless I see the mark of the nails in his hands, and put my finger in the mark of the nails and my hand in his side, I will not believe."

A week later his disciples were again in the house, and Thomas was with them. Although the doors were shut, Jesus came and stood among them and said, "Peace be with you."

Then he said to Thomas, "Put your finger here and see my hands. Reach out your hand and put it in my side. Do not doubt but believe."

Thomas answered him, "My Lord and my God!"

Jesus said to him, "Have you believed because you have seen me? Blessed are those who have not seen and yet have come to believe."

120

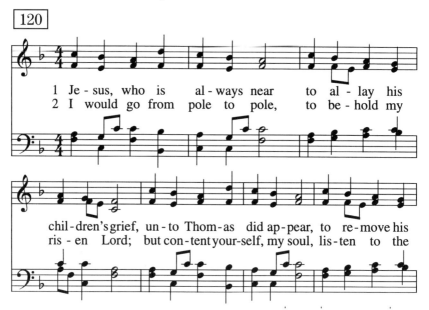

1 Je - sus, who is al - ways near to al - lay his
2 I would go from pole to pole, to be - hold my

chil - dren's grief, un - to Thom - as did ap - pear, to re - move his
ris - en Lord; but con - tent your - self, my soul, lis - ten to the

un - be - lief: "Come," he said, "My nail - prints view,
Sav - ior's word: "All who me in faith re - ceive,

and my side the sword pierced through"; hum - bled the di-
with - out see - ing still be - lieve, trust my word and

ci - ple stood, and ex - claimed, "My Lord, my God."
there - on rest, they a - bun - dant - ly are blest."

7.7.7.7.D.
GOUDIMEL (205 A)

The Appearance by the Sea
John 21:1-23

After these things Jesus showed himself again to the disciples by the Sea of Tiberias; and he showed himself in this way. Gathered there together were Simon Peter, Thomas called the Twin, Nathanael of Cana in Galilee, the sons of Zebedee, and two others of his disciples. Simon Peter said to them, "I am going fishing."

They said to him, "We will go with you."

They went out and got into the boat, but that night they caught nothing.

121 Just after daybreak, Jesus stood on the beach; but the disciples did not know that it was Jesus. Jesus said to them, "Children, you have no fish, have you?"

They answered him, "No."

He said to them, "Cast the net to the right side of the boat, and you will find some." So they cast it, and now they were not able to haul it in because there were so many fish.

That disciple whom Jesus loved said to Peter, "It is the Lord!"

When Simon Peter heard that it was the Lord, he put on some clothes, for he was naked, and jumped into the sea. But the other disciples came in the boat, dragging the net full of fish, for they were not far from the land, only about a hundred yards off.

When they had gone ashore, they saw a charcoal fire there, with fish on it, and bread.

Jesus said to them, "Bring some of the fish that you have just caught."

So Simon Peter went aboard and hauled the net ashore, full of large fish, a hundred fifty-three of them; and though there were so many, the net was not torn.

Jesus said to them, "Come and have breakfast."

Now none of the disciples dared to ask him, "Who are you?" because they knew it was the Lord.

122 Jesus came and took the bread and gave it to them, and did the same with the fish. This was now the third time that Jesus appeared to the disciples after he was raised from the dead.

When they had finished breakfast, Jesus said to Simon Peter, "Simon son of John, do you love me more than these?"

He said to him, "Yes, Lord; you know that I love you."

Jesus said to him, "Feed my lambs."

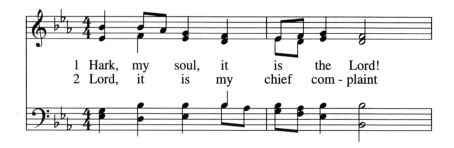

1 Hark, my soul, it is the Lord!
2 Lord, it is my chief com-plaint

Christ thy Sav-ior, hear his word: Je-sus speaks, and
that my love is weak and faint; yet I love thee

speaks to thee, "Say, poor sin-ner, lov'st thou me?"
and a-dore; O, for grace to love thee more!

7.7.7.7. Trochaic
HERRNHUT (11 A)

A second time he said to him, "Simon son of John, do you love me?"

He said to him, "Yes, Lord; you know that I love you."

Jesus said to him, "Tend my sheep."

He said to him the third time, "Simon son of John, do you love me?"

123 Peter felt hurt because he said to him the third time, "Do you love me?" And he said to him, "Lord, you know everything; you know that I love you."

Jesus said to him, "Feed my sheep."

1 How great the bliss to be a sheep of Je - sus, and
2 Who - e'er would spend their days in last-ing plea - sure must

to be guid-ed by his shep-herd-staff! Earth's great-est hon-ors,
come to Christ and join his flock with speed; here is a feast pre-

how - so - e'er they please us, com - pared to this are
pared, rich be - yond meas - ure, the world mean - while on

vain and emp - ty chaff. Yea, what this world can nev-er give, may,
emp - ty husks must feed. Those souls may share in ev-'ry good whose

through the Shep-herd's grace, each need - y sheep re - ceive.
Shep - herd does pos - sess the trea-sur-ies of God.

11.10.11.10.8.12.
AGNUS CHRISTI (115 B)

164

124 "Very truly, I tell you, when you were younger, you used to fasten your own belt and to go wherever you wished. But when you grow old, you will stretch out your hands, and someone else will fasten a belt around you and take you where you do not wish to go." (He said this to indicate the kind of death by which he would glorify God.) After this he said to him, "Follow me."

Peter turned and saw the disciple whom Jesus loved following them; he was the one who had reclined next to Jesus at the supper and had said, "Lord, who is it that is going to betray you?" When Peter saw him, he said to Jesus, "Lord, what about him?"

Jesus said to him, "If it is my will that he remain until I come, what is that to you? Follow me!"

So the rumor spread in the community that this disciple would not die. Yet Jesus did not say to him that he would not die, but, "If it is my will that he remain until I come, what is that to you?"

Long as we live, and when we die, and while in heav'n with him we reign, this song, our song of

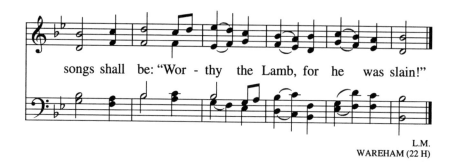

songs shall be: "Wor - thy the Lamb, for he was slain!"

L.M.
WAREHAM (22 H)

The Ascension
Matthew 28:16-20; Luke 24:52-53;
Acts 1:3-11; John 20:30-31

Now the eleven disciples went to Galilee, to the mountain to which Jesus had directed them. When they saw him, they worshiped him; but some doubted.

[125] And Jesus came and said to them, "All authority in heaven and on earth has been given to me. Go therefore and make disciples of all nations, baptizing them in the name of the Father and of the Son and of the Holy Spirit, and teaching them to obey everything that I have commanded you. And remember, I am with you always, to the end of the age."

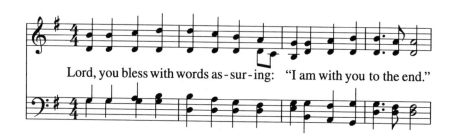

Lord, you bless with words as-sur-ing: "I am with you to the end."

Faith and hope and love re-stor-ing, may we serve as you in-tend,

and a-mid the cares that claim us, hold in mind e - ter - ni-ty;

with the Spir-it's gifts em-pow'r us for the work of min-is-try.

Jeffery Rowthorn. © Hope Publishing Company. Used by permission.

8.7.8.7.D.
HYMN TO JOY

Jesus presented himself alive to them by many convincing proofs, appearing to them during forty days and speaking about the kingdom of God. While staying with them, he ordered them not to leave Jerusalem, but to wait there for the promise of the Father. "This," he said, "is what you have heard from me; for John baptized with water, but you will be baptized with the Holy Spirit not many days from now."

126 So when they had come together, they asked him, "Lord, is this the time when you will restore the kingdom to Israel?"

He replied, "It is not for you to know the times or periods that the Father has set by his own authority. But you will receive power when the Holy Spirit has come upon you; and you will be my witnesses in Jerusalem, in all Judea and Samaria, and to the ends of the earth."

Church, go forth o'er the earth; Christ, your head, has hal'-lowed you, a cho-sen bride for-ev-er, a-dorned now for our Sav-ior; be strong and be not cheer-less, and may your saints be fear-less;

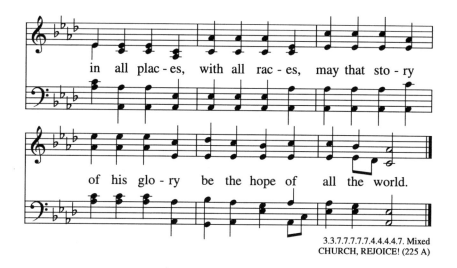

in all plac - es, with all rac - es, may that sto - ry
of his glo - ry be the hope of all the world.

3.3.7.7.7.7.4.4.4.4.7. Mixed
CHURCH, REJOICE! (225 A)

When he had said this, as they were watching, he was lifted up, and a cloud took him out of their sight. While he was going and they were gazing up toward heaven, suddenly two men in white robes stood by them. They said, "Men of Galilee, why do you stand looking up toward heaven? This Jesus, who has been taken up from you into heaven, will come in the same way as you saw him go into heaven."

| 127 | They returned to Jerusalem with great joy; and they were continually in the temple blessing God.

Now Jesus did many other signs in the presence of his disciples, which are not written in this book. But these are written so that you may come to believe that Jesus is the Messiah, the Son of God, and that through believing you may have life in his name.

8.7.8.7.D. Trochaic
CASSEL (167 A)